INDEX OF VEGETARIAN RECIPES

*Some of the recipes in this list
include stocks made from
meat/poultry – if you simply
use vegetable stock instead, the
recipe is suitable for vegetarians.
Some of the recipes contain
fish sauce.*

an oversimplified primer on fiber

Wool: Warm and elastic. Wool is an animal fiber, as are alpaca, cashmere, qiviut (musk ox), and angora. Animal fibers have a springiness and warmth that cannot be replicated with synthetic or plant-based fibers, and just like animals, each fiber has its own characteristics. Wool is too much for some people, however (they're allergic to it or they don't like how it feels against their skin), so think about that if you're knitting a gift. If allergies or itchiness aren't areas of concern, wool is perfect for knitting socks. And it's the essential ingredient if you're going to felt your knitted things (note: superwash wool will *not* felt).

Cotton: Cool and inelastic. Cotton is a plant fiber, as are flax, linen, and hemp. Until ten to fifteen years ago, most cotton for knitting was pretty nasty. Not anymore! Organic cotton, in natural shades of cream, brown, and green, is soft as a baby's tushy. I like cotton best when it's blended with something else—silk, tencel, lycra, acrylic. Beware: just because a blend is similar in makeup to another you've used does not mean that the yarn will feel or behave the same way. Some cotton-acrylic blends knit up like steel wool, others like a powder puff.

Synthetics: The new playground of the knitting world. Nothing does faux fur better than nylon. Or polyester. Plastics extruded in weird ways create soft, fuzzy textures you may never have imagined you could knit with, and yarn companies create new varieties every year. Some of the patterns in this book take advantage of them.

Go to your local yarn store (knitters call them "LYS") and browse. Contrast and compare. Covet and caress. If you find something you love the look of, buy a ball and swatch away (see page 19).

HOW TO READ A YARN LABEL

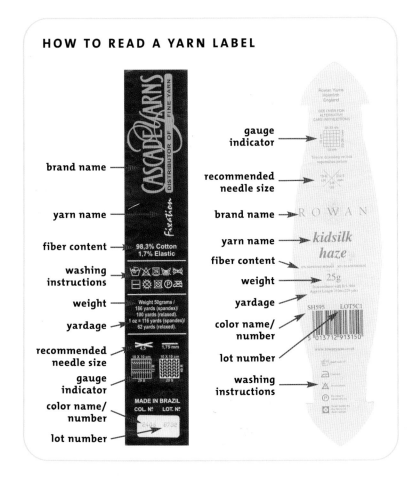

brand name
yarn name
fiber content
washing instructions
weight
yardage
recommended needle size
gauge indicator
color name/ number
lot number

gauge indicator
recommended needle size
brand name
yarn name
fiber content
weight
yardage
color name/ number
lot number
washing instructions

get your gear!

Let's start with needles. As a knitter, your needles are your best friends. Good ones make knitting easier and more enjoyable. Bad ones make you cranky.

Needles sold in North America are marked with the US or metric size–sometimes both. For example, a US #6 is the same size as a 4mm needle. A good needle-size gauge will help you be sure you're using the right size (see below).

Needles are made of plastic, metal (aluminum or steel), wood, bamboo, or casein (a plastic-like material made from dairy protein!). Straight needles come in different lengths. Circular needles are the pointy end sections of straight needles connected by a flexible cable, and also come in assorted lengths. Double-pointed needles for knitting small circular things, like socks or baby hats, come in sets of four or five.

Aluminum is slippery; bamboo has a little traction; plastic and casein are sort of in the middle. Generally, you'll find a less-slippery needle is best when you're using slippery yarn. And sticky yarns will make you crazy on anything but the smoothest needles. Experiment to see what you like best. If you want to travel with your knitting, look for airline-safe needle sets. I have one and love it.

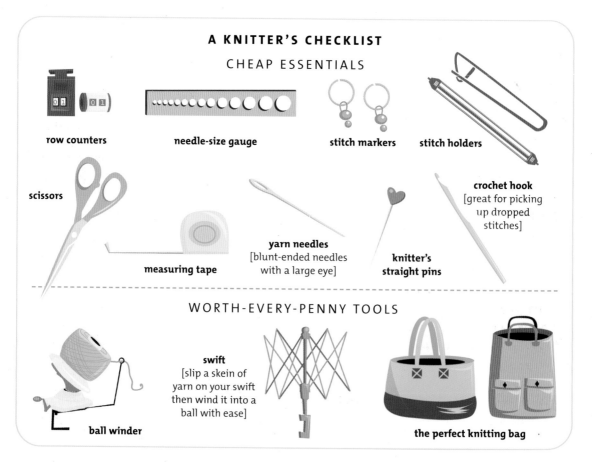

A KNITTER'S CHECKLIST

CHEAP ESSENTIALS

row counters

needle-size gauge

stitch markers

stitch holders

scissors

crochet hook
[great for picking up dropped stitches]

yarn needles
[blunt-ended needles with a large eye]

measuring tape

knitter's straight pins

WORTH-EVERY-PENNY TOOLS

ball winder

swift
[slip a skein of yarn on your swift then wind it into a ball with ease]

the perfect knitting bag

Most knitters build their collection a set of needles at a time. If they don't already have the size, length, or type they need for their next project, they get them when they buy the yarn.

After years of experimentation with every type of needle, circulars have become my needles of choice. I now knit exclusively on them, except when double-pointed needles (DPNs) are necessary. The most important thing in a circular needle is the join. If it's rough or bumpy, you'll have to fight to get the work past it every few minutes and it will ruin the fun of knitting. Look for lightweight circulars with smooth joins.

THE KNITTING BAG: A KNITTER'S FAVORITE TOOL

You want it:

* big enough to hold your project, plus needles, extra yarn, tools
* sturdy and strong, so that needles won't poke through the bag
* to have a comfortable handle or strap for carrying
* to open wide so you can get at everything easily

You'd like it:

* waterproof so that you can set it at your feet anywhere, even messy places
* if not waterproof, at least washable
* full of little pockets for your tools so you can find them again

You probably don't want it:

* to have closures that will snag your yarn, like rough zippers or Velcro
* to be heavy when empty
* to look threatening in any way, if you plan to take it on an airplane!

What about straight needles? I will state this categorically, backed up by my knitting friends *and* the entire country of Norway: you do not need straight needles to knit, ever. (They only sell circulars and DPNs in knitter-loving Norway, you know.) Circulars can be used to knit something in the round, like a tube, but you can also knit back and forth on them as if they were a pair of straight needles.

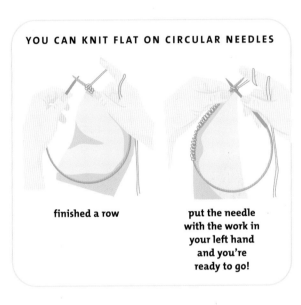

YOU CAN KNIT FLAT ON CIRCULAR NEEDLES

finished a row

put the needle with the work in your left hand and you're ready to go!

How? If you knit on two straight needles, you're only concerned with the two pointy ends, right? Well, when you use a circular needle, you hold one point in each hand and ignore the middle section.

After you finish a row, simply turn the work around so that the needle you held in your left hand is now in your right. You're ready to work the next row. Ta-da!

There's another advantage to circulars. With straights, you have to hold the work up with each stitch. Circulars are so much easier on your wrists. Your lap carries the weight instead.

IT'S TIME FOR YOUR FIRST LESSON

casting on

There are a lot of ways to get the yarn on the needle. The laziest is to ask a knitter to do it for you. But eventually you're going to have to do it yourself.

Smidge of advice: read through the next section before you try it.

Casting on is not so hard. First, get some smooth yarn (fuzz will only make it harder to see what you're doing) and a set of knitting needles that matches the size called for on the yarn's label.

There are many ways to cast on. Some get the yarn onto your needle easily but make the first row harder to knit (the e-wrap cast on, for example). An

> **OUR FAVORITE LEARN-TO-KN!T YARNS**
> **Wool:** Cascade 220, Rowan Magpie
> **Cotton/blend:** Mission Falls 1824 cotton, Lion Brand Cotton-Ease

annoying first row puts anyone in a bad mood, so I'm going to teach you my favorite all-purpose cast on. It might be a little trickier to learn, but it's much easier to knit from and is quite stable.

For the moment, you only need one needle, so put the other aside. (Now is not the time to use circular needles.)

TO CAST ON:

A. Make a slip knot and slide it over the pointy end of the needle. Make sure to leave a long, long tail (the tail is the part that's not attached to the ball of yarn.) This is unsurprisingly called the *long-tail cast-on.*

B. Hold the needle firmly in your right hand. You now need to hold the yarn in a very specific way: Grab both strands of yarn with your left hand, making sure the long tail is at the back. Insert your pointer finger and thumb between the strands to separate them and hold the strands with your three free fingers (the thumb and pointer are now busy holding the yarn taut). The right hand's only job is to hold the needle. Don't let go!

C. Now tilt your other hand out toward the left till your palm faces the sky. A loop begins to form around your thumb. Take the knitting needle in your right hand and move it toward your body; that will close the loop.

(continued)

D. Now take the tip of the needle and slip it into the loop from underneath.

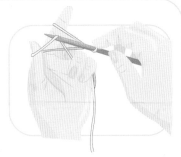

E. Get the yarn on your pointer finger—you've just gone *under* the loop so now you go *over* the yarn on your pointer finger, looping it around the needle.

F. Hold the right needle firmly and pivot your left wrist to the right until your needle tip passes back through the thumb

loop. Your entire left hand is now sitting behind the needle. Now drop your thumb so the yarn slips off it, flick that thumb to the front, and push forward the strand of yarn that's hanging down.

G. Spread your thumb and pointer finger apart to tighten the loose yarn. A little rocking motion helps snug it up nicely.

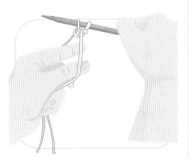

You have made a stitch.

Okay, has your brain seized up? Too much to absorb? Stay cool. Go back and try again, and follow each step slowly and deliberately. This is like cat's cradle, except the resulting loops get captured on your knitting needle, one after another.

Cast on as many stitches as you can before you run out of yarn in your long tail. Most reputable sources say you'll need 1 inch of yarn per stitch you cast on, plus a little extra. The thicker your yarn, the more "extra" you'll need. So if you're casting on 100 stitches, your tail needs to be at least 100 inches long. What happens if you run short? The only remedy is to rip back, add more yarn to your long tail, and start again. So measure first. It just takes a few extra seconds and prevents frustration.

Work so that each cast-on stitch is about the same distance from the next. Give each stitch a bit of breathing space. And don't overtighten them on the needle, or you'll have to fight to knit the first row. If you find you can't loosen up, cast on to a needle a size larger than what is called for in the pattern. Now work your first row with the correct size needle in your left hand and you'll have just enough ease so that you're not pulling your hair out with each stitch. (When you get to the second row, don't forget to switch *that* needle to the correct size as well.)

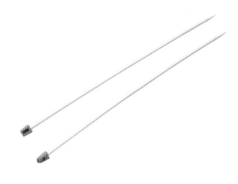

HOW TO TELL RIGHT FROM WRONG

When you finish casting on using the long-tail method, the first row you will knit is actually the *wrong* side. Yes, knitting has sides. **In something knit in stockinette stitch, one side looks like little interlocking Vs and the other side is an endless sea of horizontal bumps.** The bumpy side is the wrong side.

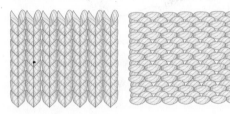

But how can you tell in a tiny cast-on row? Look at it closely. On one side, the stitches create a row of horizontal bumps at the base of the work (below the needle).

On the other side, you find pretty, angled stitches that snuggle politely together.

Just remember: Pretty = front. (Of course, designers play with this all the time, so don't assume. *Always read your pattern carefully.*)

the knit stitch

To make your life easier, we're going to knit in garter stitch for a while. This means you knit every row. You will get a fabric that has bumps on both sides, and it can look really neat. A few patterns in this book, like the Jelly scarf and the Freak vest, use just garter stitch. What are you going to make first? Let's call it your knitter's training wheels. You're going to experiment and practice on this piece, so don't fuss about how it looks.

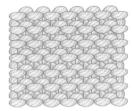

garter stitch

RULE NUMBER 1: **You only wrap the yarn around the needle in your right hand.** Whether you're knitting or purling, this is true. If you get confused, just remember: [w]rap = right.

The left hand holds the work when you begin a new row, so put the needle with the cast-on stitches in your left hand. You'll notice that the long tail is much shorter now and is sitting in the front. Ignore it*. From now on, you're only going to deal with the strand of yarn that's attached to the ball—the *working* yarn.

* *I lied. On the very first stitch of your first row, you will need to tug the remains of the long tail to tighten the first stitch—you loosened it when you stuck the right-hand needle into it the first time. You just need to do this once and that's it.*

WHICH SIDE OF THE OCEAN DO YOU KNIT ON?

Continental knitters hold the yarn and form stitches with their left hand. What I do (and what I've written about in this book) is called American or English knitting, which involves wrapping each stitch with your right hand. There is also something called "combination knitting," which uses bits of both methods. What should you do? Do what feels most comfortable. There is no wrong way to knit if the finished product pleases you.

GET LOOPY

Each stitch is really a vertical loop that sits over the needle, right? Look at one stitch closely and you'll notice that **one side of the loop sits slightly more forward—closer to the tip of the needle— than the other.**

You should always work with the side of the loop that is sitting forward (unless the pattern instructs otherwise, as in "k tbl"—knit through the *back* of the loop).

Why? Because the loops naturally want to lean slightly in one direction. If you work with the part of the loop that sits behind, you'll be twisting your stitches as you knit. Again, sometimes the pattern *tells you* to twist your stitches, but mostly you won't

want this. **(If the right side of your stockinette stitch looks like little Xs instead of little Vs, you're twisted.)**

Does this mean you have to stare at every single freaking stitch before you knit it? Don't be silly. You can usually assume that the forward-sitting side of the loop is on the side of the needle that's closest to your body—the *front* of the loop, it's called. But not always. If you accidentally drop a stitch, you can easily pick it up twisted without meaning to. So understanding the way the loops sit on the needle will make your life easier.

An awesome body of knowledge in a friendly package: The people at your LYS can be a huge help when you're learning new knitting stuff. If you've bought the yarn or the pattern (or this book!) at their shop, don't be shy about asking for help with things you don't understand. (I learned how to do cables from someone who worked at my LYS.) If you can't find someone friendly, find a new yarn shop. Most staffers are eager to help you, because they're knitters too!

THE KNIT STITCH:

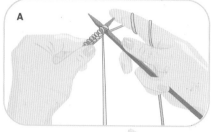

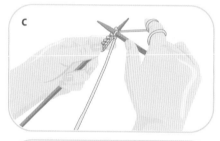

A. Hold the second (empty) knitting needle and the working yarn in your right hand. Almost everyone does this differently. Here's what I do: I'm right handed, so I hold the right needle with my thumb and all my fingers except my pointer finger. That finger is my tension and stitch-making finger. I wrap the working yarn (remember: the strand that's attached to the ball) around my pointer finger twice and hold it up a little so that the yarn isn't flapping about as I move my needles.

Now, with the yarn behind the RH (right-hand) needle, slip the tip of the RH needle from *left to right* into the front of the stitch. The RH needle sits *behind* the LH (left-hand) needle. You want about an inch of needle tip to be sticking out past the stitch, so that your work doesn't fall off in your hands. You'll soon come to know what feels right.

B. Wrap the yarn from back to front around the RH needle tip. Hold the RH needle and yarn taut and pull the RH needle gently to the right. Look closely and you'll see the stitch forming on the *front* of the RH needle.

C. Continue pulling the RH needle to the right until you can pass the RH needle's tip forward and to the left again, *in front of* the LH needle. This catches the stitch.

D. Continue to push the RH needle forward so a good inch of RH needle tip is overlapping the LH needle. Now all you do is slide the RH needle to the right and the completed stitch will fall onto the RH needle where it belongs.

This will feel, for a while, like you're trying to floss your teeth with your toes. Do not be discouraged. We all felt like that in the beginning. Stick with it and it will get easier. And while you're learning, ignore your mistakes and just work at understanding how to make each stitch. Soon, you will make fewer mistakes. Later on, I'll show you how to fix some of the most common ones.

Now what? Just knit each stitch until you reach the end of the row. Then take the work, which is in your right hand, and put it in your left. Begin your second row just as you began the first. Then keep going!

the purl stitch

If you knit only using the knit stitch, which is what we've just done, you get garter stitch. It's fun, casual-looking, and lays pretty flat. That's why it's great for scarves.

If you want to knit something a little more elegant, you need to learn to purl. This is *not* a big deal. You hear me? It's not.

The combination of knitted rows and purled rows gives you stockinette stitch. You knit one row (the front) and purl the next (the back). Purling is exactly

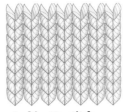

stockinette stitch

like knitting, except that you are working on a different side of the loop, from a slightly different angle.

Ready? Okay. Take your training-wheels piece, which is probably rows and rows of knit stitches by now. Make sure you're ready to start a new row. Hold the work in your left hand, as usual, with the empty needle in your right hand, and you're ready to begin.

THE PURL STITCH:

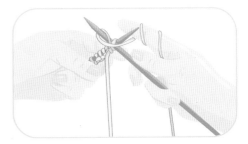

A. **With the yarn in front of the RH needle, slip the tip of the RH needle from *right to left* into the front of the first stitch.** The RH needle sits *in front* of the LH needle.

B. **Wrap the yarn from back to front around the RH needle tip.** Hold the RH needle and yarn taut and pull the RH needle gently to the right until you can pass the RH needle's tip back and to the left again, slipping *behind* the LH needle. This catches the stitch. Continue to push the RH needle forward and slide it to the right. The completed stitch will fall onto the RH needle where it belongs.

Not so mysterious, really. Finish this row with purl stitches only, then switch back to knit stitches on the next row, and then back to purl again. Continue alternating between one knitted and one purled row for a while. Notice that once you've knit a good section of stockinette stitch, it will start to curl in at the sides. But the stockinette fabric is very pretty.

That's the trade off. And when stockinette-stitch pieces are blocked (see page 19) and seamed into a garment, side-seam curling usually isn't an issue anymore. (When you knit a piece entirely in stockinette stitch, the hem will roll up as well. That's why you often see more stable stitches like ribbing or garter at the hem or cuffs of garments—they don't roll!)

INCREASING AND DECREASING

To create shape in a knitted item, you increase (create more stitches) or decrease (combine stitches). There are a lot of different kinds of increases and decreases. Some are angled to the left, some to the right, some are nearly invisible, some leave just a little evidence that you've used them—like a tiny horizontal bar. Very often, a pattern will call for a specific increase or decrease, because carefully placed increases or decreases can be very decorative. Look at Banff's raglan shaping (pg 98), for example—it's beautiful!

Sally Melville's *The Knitting Experience* series is an excellent resource to help you learn these techniques and tons of others. In fact, you may want a selection of good knitting books to refer to, since every knitter/writer teaches stuff in their own way. Time to head back to the LYS!

the bind off

If you've been practicing knit and purl stitches on your training-wheels piece for many many rows, as you should, you're probably sick of looking at the thing. You want to start fresh, now that you're a little more sure of your skills. What do you do when you need to get knitted work off the needles without it unraveling into a messy tangle? You bind off.

For the prettiest look, bind off in the same stitch pattern you're working. So if it's stockinette stitch and it's time for a knit row when you reach the bind-off point, you'll knit each stitch as you bind off.

THE BIND OFF:

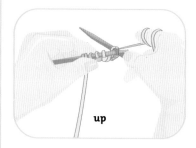
up

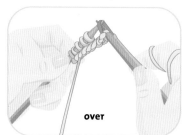
over

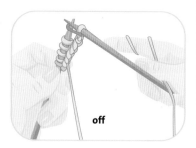
off

To bind off, work the first two stitches in pattern. Stop. Take your LH needle, slip the tip into the front of the stitch on the far right of the RH needle [the 1st stitch you worked], lift it *up,* pull it *over* the second stitch, and let it drop *off* the RH needle. See how it locks itself around the base of the second stitch? That's the idea. Now work another stitch. Again, take the stitch that's farthest right and again, lift it *up, over* the stitch to its left, and *off* the needle. Keep working one more stitch and then lifting the farthest right stitch *up, over,* and *off* the needle until you're on the very last stitch. Pull on this stitch to loosen it, making it much larger. Cut a foot or so of yarn from the ball, pass the cut end through the last stitch, and pull the cut end to secure it. **Shake my hand. You're one of us now.**

you can read a pattern

Now that you can knit and purl, you know almost everything necessary to follow any pattern. No, seriously. Stop looking at me like that.

All you need to do now is to learn the language. For example, when you see "k1, p1," that means knit one stitch, purl one stitch. Very often, instructions are repeated, and when that happens, you will see the repeated section surrounded by asterisks or brackets. Like this: *k1, p1*, repeat till end. That means k1, p1, k1, p1 (over and over) until you reach the end of the row. A repeated pattern of knit and purl stitches in the same row creates ribbing. K1, p1 makes a skinny rib. K4, p2 makes a wide rib with a skinny space between. Experiment!

What does "work" mean? Patterns say "work" when they want to instruct you to continue knitting without specifying the exact stitch you're to make. So if you're to "*work* next 10 rows in pattern," that just means follow the pattern as established for the next 10 rows. When a pattern says "*knit* next 10 rows," it means knit every stitch for the next 10 rows. Finicky, this knitting stuff, eh?

Most abbreviations used in patterns are identified in a list somewhere *in* the pattern book or magazine. You'll see our list on page 24. Each abbreviation is followed by a full-text explanation. If the abbreviation isn't a common one, you should also find a description of what you're supposed to do.

TWO ESSENTIAL THINGS TO REMEMBER ABOUT PATTERNS

1. **Some patterns are written clearly and are easy to follow.** Others, not so much. So before you start knitting a pattern, sit down and scan it. Look for important directions like "at the same time" and highlight them in some way, so you won't miss them later. When you're working a pattern, read the section ahead before you start knitting it. If there's something you can't figure out on your own, ask an experienced knitter or your friendly LYS person.

2. **Patterns are written by people. People make mistakes.** The people who write knitting patterns have a lot of systems in place to catch errors before they're printed. Test knitters, technical editors, and proofreaders all work toward pattern perfection, but mistakes happen. So before you start a new pattern, check the website of the publisher of the book or magazine and look for "Errata." You'll find fixes to any known errors in published patterns there. (The errata page for *Knit Wit* can be found here: http://amysinger.ca/knitwit)

janda hoodie

DESIGNED BY AMY SWENSON

A hoodie is now as
essential a wardrobe staple as
a pair of jeans has always been. This version is as
comfy as an old sweatshirt but with twice the style.
Janda has the requisite hood but skips the front
pouch pocket, so you can bypass the shlub look and
go straight to sporty. Knit a body-skimming size for a
slinky fit, or go up a few sizes for baggy but beautiful.

Difficulty: ⬤ 4

SIZE
S[M, L, XL, XXL]

FINISHED MEASUREMENTS
Chest: 38[42, 46, 51, 55]"
Length: 21[21, 22, 23, 24]"

MATERIALS
(MC) Mission Falls 1824 Wool (100% wool;
84yd/77m per 50g); color: 028 Pistachio;
7[7, 8, 9, 10] skeins

(CC1) Mission Falls 1824 Wool; color: 022 Ink;
8[8, 9, 10, 11] skeins
(CC2) Mission Falls 1824 Wool; color: 001 Natural; 1 skein
2 US #6/4 mm circular needle
1 US #7/4.5 mm circular needle
1 US G/4 mm crochet hook
Stitch markers
Yarn needle

GAUGE
18 sts/24 rows = 4" in St st on larger needles

knit wit
102

STITCH PATTERNS

SINGLE DEC ROW:
K1, ssk, work to last 3 sts, k2tog, k1.
(2 fewer sts on needle)

PATTERN

BACK:
With MC and smaller needles, CO 85[95, 105,
115, 125] sts.
Work in 3x2 Rib for 2", ending with RS facing.
Change to larger needles and work in St st until piece
measures 12.5[12.5, 13, 13.5, 14]" from beg, ending
with RS facing. BO 4[5, 7, 7, 9] sts at beg
of next 2 rows. (77[85, 91, 101, 107] sts)

FRONT:
Work as for back. *At the same time*, when 43[51, 51,
53, 53] sts rem on needle, P1 row, then begin shaping
neck while continuing raglan dec as est.
To shape neck, work first 21[25, 25, 26, 26] sts as

est, attach second ball of MC, BO 1 st, work rem
21[25, 25, 26, 26] sts.
Dec 1 st each side of neckline on next and foll 8
rows, then work neckline even, continuing raglan dec
as est.

SLEEVES (make two):
With CC1 and smaller needles, CO 45[50, 50,
55, 55] sts.
Work in 3x2 Rib for 2", ending with RS facing.
Change to larger needles. K1, inc 1[0, 0, 1, 1] sts,
work 18[21, 21, 23, 23] sts, PM, work Inset Rib
Patt, PM, work 20[22, 22, 25, 25] sts.
(46[50, 50, 56, 56] sts)
Work even, maintaining Inset Rib Patt, until piece
measures 5" from beg.

FINISHING

Block pieces to size and sew raglan seams.
Sew side and sleeve seams.

knit wit
103

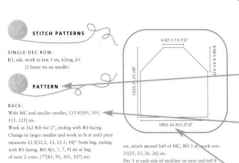

6.5[7, 7, 7.5, 7.5]"

8.5[8.5, 9, 9.5, 9.5]"

21[21.2, 23, 24]"

19[21, 23, 25.5, 27.5]"

knit wit

Instead of lugging around an entire book or
magazine, make *one* photocopy of the pattern
you're using. You can even enlarge those teeny
tiny charts, make notes, fold it up, and cross out
parts you've finished. It weighs nothing!
But only make copies of patterns you
own to respect copyright law.

Read **the intro text** to learn about why the designer created the pattern and look for tips that make knitting it easier.

This picture isn't just for pretty. Look at it closely. Do you like the design features? Will it look good on you?

Sizes differ from pattern to pattern, so always check the finished measurements to see if the thing will fit. The smallest size is listed first, with larger sizes following in brackets. When you get to the pattern instructions, use the number in the same position in the brackets as the size you're knitting.

Finished measurements correspond to the sizes above. Pick the measurement that gives you the amount of ease you want; 2" is close fitting, 6" is oversized.

Your shopping list—take the pattern with you to the yarn shop.

If your gauge matches these numbers, your knitted thing will be the size you expected it to be. See page 19. Sometimes the gauge indicator asks for gauge in a specific pattern—like garter stitch.

The pattern is written in a specific order. Start at the top and work, step by step, until you reach the end. You'll see headings for each part of the pattern like "body" or "sleeves" as you go.

See? **The smaller size** is first, followed by the larger sizes in brackets. Circle the size you're making right on the pattern to make it easier to follow.

Schematics show the finished measurements of each piece of the pattern, for each size.

When you get here, you're almost done! But don't skimp on **the finishing**...careful seams and neatly woven-in ends make your knitted thing look extra great.

In this book, you'll find each **designer's favorite knitting secret** at the end of the pattern. Cool.

YOU'RE IN CONTROL

gauge and swatching

What's gauge? Gauge is the number of stitches (width) and rows (length) per inch. It sounds deadly dull, but it's actually essential knowledge if you want the stuff you knit to turn out like you planned.

GAUGE IS CONTROLLED BY THREE FACTORS:

1. **the yarn you use**

   How thick or thin it is, how it knits up, how it behaves after washing and blocking.

2. **the needles you use**

   Thinner needles create more stitches per inch; thicker needles create fewer stitches per inch.

3. **your own tension**

   You have tension? All knitters do. The way you hold your yarn and wrap your stitches—and even your mood—will affect the final product.

So how do you deal with gauge? You make a swatch before you begin each project. It shows you how the yarn knits up before you commit to the whole thing. Most importantly, it helps you make something that will fit, so it won't end up permanently hidden behind your laundry basket.

To swatch, use your chosen yarn and the needle size called for in the pattern. Cast on the number of stitches called for in the gauge indicator + 10 (for example, if the pattern's gauge is 18 stitches over 4 inches, cast on 28 stitches). Work the swatch in the pattern called for in the gauge indicator: stockinette, cable, whatever. This isn't negotiable.

When your swatch is at least 5 inches tall, bind off. If the gauge indicator says the gauge is taken *after blocking*, this means you have to treat the swatch as if it were a finished garment. That might mean washing and drying your swatch as directed on the yarn's label. If you're using non-superwash wool, it's a little more complicated: dampen the swatch with water, give it one good vertical tug, lay it down, and pin it flat without distorting its shape.

ALL FLUFF IS NOT CREATED EQUAL

Using the yarn called for in the pattern is the easiest way to get a predictable result. Designers take a lot of things into consideration when choosing yarn—things like thickness, loft, texture, elasticity, color, sheen.

But *you don't always have to use the yarn specified.* Just do your research and don't fall in love based on color alone. Take the pattern to your favorite LYS people and pick their brains. They'll help you find a suitable substitute. And then swatch before you begin. Promise me. Swatch first? Good.

Let it dry. When the swatch is completely dry, unpin it, leave it to relax a few minutes (it may have shrunk during the drying process), and then take your gauge reading as follows:

Measure the number of stitches across 4 inches. Take your measurement in a few different sections of the swatch, to make sure it's accurate. If you consistently find a half stitch at the end of your 4-inch section, include that half stitch. Let's say you've found 20.5 stitches. Now count how many rows are in 4 vertical inches of your swatch. Let's say you counted 28 rows. The gauge you worked is 20.5/28.

I HAVE MY GAUGE...NOW WHAT?

If your number is exactly the same as the gauge in the pattern, you are a lucky knitter. You can proceed!

If your number is *smaller* than the gauge called for in the pattern, you have **fewer** stitches per inch than you need. If you knit the pattern using this yarn and needle combination, your knitted thing will be **bigger** than you want in all directions. Feh.

The I-have-too-few-stitches fix:

✳ Knit a new swatch with a needle one size smaller.
   If this makes the knitted fabric too stiff...
✳ Choose a thinner yarn.

If your number is *bigger* than the gauge called for, you have **more** stitches than you need. If you knit the pattern using this yarn and needle combination, your knitted thing will be **smaller** than you want in all directions. Also feh.

The I-have-too-many-stitches fix:

✳ Knit a new swatch with a needle one size larger.
   If this makes the knitted fabric too floppy...
✳ Choose a thicker yarn.

It is completely possible that you won't end up using the needle size called for in the pattern even if you use the same yarn, and that's just fine. **The gauge you achieve with your combination of needle and yarn is what counts; if it matches the gauge in the pattern, it's correct.** Really. Just keep adjusting your needle size until you get gauge. And if you just can't get gauge, it's time to change the yarn, too.

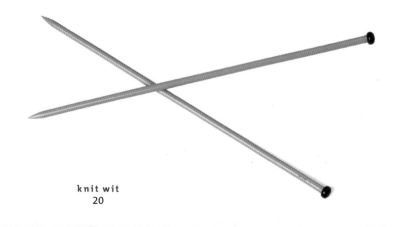

YOU'RE NEW AT THIS

So now what? You know the basics and are ready to try something more than your training-wheels piece. My prescription? Knit a 6-foot-long garter stitch scarf. Don't roll your eyes at me, you. The way to get really good at knitting and build your confidence is to do a lot of it, over and over.

Go to your LYS (this is the fun part!) and get about 500 to 600 yards of smooth worsted or aran-weight yarn. Variegated yarns (yarns that incorporate a whole bunch of colors) are best for this project. The built-in color changes will keep you amused as you knit and knit and knit. And knit.

Cast on about 30 stitches: more if for thinner yarn, fewer for thicker. Make a scarf any width you like—aim for at least 6 inches. Knit each row until the first ball of yarn is gone, and then attach another.

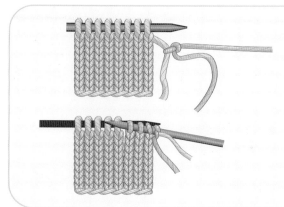

TIE ONE ON!

When you start a new ball of yarn, it looks tidier if you make the change at the beginning of a row. Loosely tie the old yarn to the new yarn with a single knot and leave several inches of yarn tails hanging. Knit a few stitches, then go back and adjust and tighten the knot so that it's as smooth and flat as possible. You'll weave in the ends when you've finished the scarf. Use the same technique when you change colors for stripes!

When you finish a row, hold up your work and check for little errors that you can fix before they get bigger. But you don't always have to fix every mistake. Sometimes you can make a bigger mess trying to make something perfect than if you just left it alone.

When you get to the end of 6 feet or are close to running out of yarn, bind off all stitches. A 6-foot-long scarf is a very handy accessory, but—bonus!—knitting it gives your hands and fingers time to memorize the movements of knitting. When you're done, you may want to knit another 6-footer, but you don't have to. You're ready to move on up!

For your next project, pick a pattern labeled "easy" or "for beginners" with simple, clear instructions. Read through it and be sure it makes sense to you. If you ask me *what* to knit, I'd say choose something that you can't wait to wear. Look at the pattern picture frequently as you knit. Imagine yourself in the thing. This will keep you going. When picking the size to knit, measure a similar garment that fits you well and whatever size is closest to those measurements, that's the size you should knit.

For now, just knit for yourself. Only you should be subjected to your learning curve. And only you will really appreciate the work that went into every stitch.

AVOID NEW-KNITTER BOOBY TRAPS

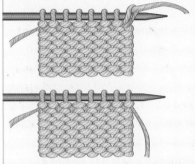

The dreaded accidental increase: You'll notice your work gets one stitch larger at the beginning of some rows. How? When you begin a row, the first stitch can look like two stitches if the working yarn is flipped **behind** the needle. Simply lift the working yarn up and over the needle so that it's sitting in **front** before you begin to work and the fake-out double stitch turns back into a well-behaved single stitch. Whew.

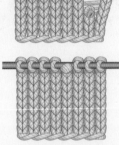

Dropping stitches: As you knit, it's very easy for a single stitch to slip unnoticed from your LH needle. You'll see it either as a ladder of stitches running down your work or, if you catch it quickly, the single loop of the stitch that's fallen off. To fix each dropped stitch, slip the tip of your crochet hook through the dropped stitch, reach through and grab the horizontal bar of yarn that looks out of place, then pull that through and slip it on the LH needle. This can be finicky, because you must be sure to pick up the stitch from the correct side of the work depending on whether you're knitting or purling. (A quick hands-on tutorial with your favorite knitter or LYS staffer will help you get the hang of it.)

Incomplete stitches: If you wrap a stitch but don't complete it, you'll eventually (usually on the following row) find the wrap sitting on the right of the stitch, with the old stitch still sitting on the needle. To fix, go back and pull the wrap up and over the stitch and off the needle.

Double-wrapping stitches: When you're distracted, it's easy to accidentally wrap the yarn twice around the needle. You'll notice you've made this error when you get to the same stitch on the next row and the accidental extra wrap drops off the needle, leaving a big, loose stitch. The only fix is to rip back your work to that original double-wrapped stitch, wrap it properly, and then continue as normal.

The difference between an experienced knitter and an inexperienced knitter is not mistakes. *All knitters make mistakes.* But the experienced knitter knows how to avoid them, how to spot them if they can't be avoided, and most importantly, how to fix them.

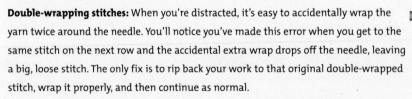

you're ready for more

There is so much to know in knitting, and the best thing is that you can take in as much or as little as you want. You never have to knit a sweater if you don't want to. But the first time you do something new and it works, like turning the heel of a sock or neatly mattress stitching your first raglan seam, you feel really, really smart.

I learn from books and magazines and websites. But mostly, I learn from my knitting friends. We get together every week or two, order coffee, talk way too loud, and share what we've been working on since we saw each other last. What they're knitting gets me thinking about what I'd like to do next. Their successes give me confidence to try new things.

If you don't know anyone who knits, look for a **knitting guild** or **"stitch & bitch"** group in your town and drop by—you'll find listings online. **Teach a friend to knit** and form a group of two. And visit us at Knitty.com for inspiration any time you need a lift, something new to knit, or help with a technique that's really bugging you. We're open 24/7.

Mostly, just knit. The more there are of us, the better this world will be. Cue the violins and dancing frog. I'm going yarn shopping.

WHAT DO YOU WANT TO KNIT?

finally. the projects! wahoo!

A fine bunch of designers and I came up with the following assortment of knitted delights. Some of them are silly, some are sexy, and some are surprising. We hope you like.

Here and on the next page, you'll find the keys to reading the patterns that follow. All abbreviations used in the patterns are listed to the right, so you'll be able to crack the code. Techniques you need to know follow the abbreviations, and then it's on to the good stuff!

LEVELS OF DIFFICULTY

These icons appear next to every project to indicate their challenge quotient.

* Simple pattern, shaping, stitches

* Simple pattern, more stitches
* A little more focus required

0 3

* More involved pattern, more techniques to grasp, trickier stitches

0 4

* Fully styled pattern
* More complex instructions
* Solid finishing skills required

ABBREVIATIONS

alt	alternate	**p**	purl
approx	approximately	**p2tog**	purl two together
beg	begin(ning)	**patt**	pattern(s)
bet	between	**PM**	place marker
BO	bind off (cast off)	**psso**	pass slipped stitch(es) over
CC	contrasting color	**rem**	remaining
circ	circular needle	**rep**	repeat
CO	cast on	**rev St st**	reverse stockinette stitch
cont	continue(ing)		
dec	decrease(ing)	**RH**	right hand
div	divide	**RS**	right side(s)
DPN	double-pointed needle(s)	**rnd**	round(s)
est	established	**sc**	single crochet
foll	follow(s)(ing)	**skp**	slip, knit, psso
g	gram(s)	**ssk**	slip, slip, knit
inc	increase(ing)	**ssp**	slip, slip, purl
incl	include(ing)	**sl**	slip
inst	instructions	**sl st**	slip stitch
k	knit	**st(s)**	stitch(es)
kfb	knit into front and back of stitch	**St st**	stockinette stitch
k2tog	knit two together	**tbl**	through back of loop(s)
LH	left hand	**tog**	together
m	meter(s)	**WYIB**	with yarn in back
MC	main color	**WYIF**	with yarn in front
m1	make one stitch	**WS**	wrong side(s)
mm	millimeter(s)	**yd**	yard(s)
mult	multiple	**YO**	yarn over
opp	opposite	** **	repeat directions between ** as indicated
oz	ounce(s)		

techniques you need to know

3-needle BO Used to join two knit pieces together. Hold work (each piece on its own needle) with both RSs facing each other, needles parallel. Insert RH needle into first stitch of each piece, wrap as for a regular knit stitch, and complete stitch. (It's awkward, but you'll get the hang of it.) When you have knit two stitches, BO as usual. Continue to knit together and then BO, stitch by stitch, until last stitch. Break yarn and thread through last stitch.

felting/fulling The intentional shrinking of a knitted wool thing–properly called "fulling," but commonly referred to as "felting." Set washing machine to normal cycle, hot, low water level. Add a small bit of soap or rinse-free wool wash and an old pair of colorfast jeans (warning: they may get stained) for extra agitation. To reduce felting fuzz that can clog washer drain, put the knitted thing into a zippered pillowcase or lingerie bag. If the water starts to cool, drain and start cycle again. Felting can happen almost instantly, or take forever—as many as three to four wash cycles. Stay close and monitor progress frequently. When you can no longer see individual stitches, drain the water and advance to the spin cycle. There is no need to rinse if you have used rinse-free wool wash. Spin excess water out of item and remove from washer immediately. Follow blocking/drying instructions in the specific pattern you're using.

garter st Knit every row. To count rows in garter stitch, one ridge = two rows.

I-cord A knitted tube. *Knit 1 row. Do not turn. Slide sts to R end of needle and k next row.* Every few rows, tug to even the tube. Repeat until tube is desired length.

reverse stockinette Purl the RS rows, knit the WS rows. To count rows in reverse stockinette stitch, one bump = one row.

make one Also called a lifted increase. To make one stitch: lift the horizontal bar between stitches, twist it, and place it on the LH needle.

mattress st A way to invisibly seam two finished knit pieces together. See the step-by-step tutorial with photos here: http://knitty.com/ISSUEspring04/mattress.html

pick up (and knit) To pick up, slip the tip of your needle through the work, wrap yarn around needle as if to knit, pull yarn through to the front to form a stitch and leave on RH needle.

   To pick up and knit, pick up stitch as above, knit it and leave on RH needle before picking up next stitch.

ssk Slip two stitches (as if to knit) to RH needle, knit two stitches together with LH needle.

ssp Slip two stitches (as if to purl) to RH needle, purl two stitches together with LH needle.

stockinette stitch Knit the RS rows, purl the WS rows. To count rows in stockinette stitch, one V = one row.

you're
a little
chilly

WHAT, ARE YOU COLD?
Here.
You could make a nice hat
so your head won't freeze.
And something for around your neck.
Your nose looks cold, too.
So knit this.
Isn't that better?

postmodern legwarmers ✳ rockstar scarf ✳ free-standing muffler
coif ✳ pixie hat ✳ nosewarmer, 2nd generation ✳ sacred & profane
convertibles ✳ dreadlock hat ✳ third-eye chullo ✳ fuzzy feet redux

postmodern legwarmers

DESIGNED BY STEFANIE JAPEL

It's not that legwarmers are "in" or "out": it's what they look like and how you wear them that matters. These are just too good to pass up. Light-as-air hand-dyed mohair is whipped into a toasty-warm froth that you can show or hide—your choice. Tied with bows at the top, they're pretty enough to show off with a skirt. Or slip them under your pants and let only the flared bottoms peek out over the tops of your shoes. How sly are you?

THE BASIC PATTERN CAN BE ALTERED IN A MULTITUDE OF WAYS. Use smaller needles and a fine, stretchy yarn, and add two or three inches of ribbing at the top—but keep the finished dimensions the same. Substitute elastic for the knitted cord. Hem the bottoms or not. Add a pattern stitch, like cables or lace, up the sides. Decorate with intarsia or a Fair Isle band. Make them thigh-high or ankle-length. Go nuts!

SIZE

S[M, L]

FINISHED MEASUREMENTS

Circumference: 10[12, 14]", unstretched
Length: 9[11, 11]"

MATERIALS

Lorna's Laces Glory (mohair blend;
120yd/110m per 50g); color: Icehouse; 3 skeins

1 set US #15/10 mm straight needles
1 set US #11/8 mm straight needles
1 set US #8/5 mm straight needles
Yarn needle

GAUGE

11 sts/12 rows = 4" in St st on largest needles

PATTERN

LEGWARMER (make two):
With US #11/8 mm needles, CO 23[25, 27] sts.
Work 4 rows even in St st.
Next row (turning ridge): P.
Next row: change to largest needles and work
even in St st for 7 rows.
Next row: Inc 1 st each side. (25[27, 29] sts)
Work even in St st for 7[9, 9]" from beg, ending
with RS facing.
Next row: (K3, m1) 7 times, k4. (32[34, 36] sts)
Work 7 rows even in St st.
Next row: (K4, m1) 7 times, k4. (39[41, 43] sts)
Work even until work measures 10(12, 12)" from
beg, ending with RS facing.
Next row (turning ridge): P.
Work 4 rows even in St st.

CORD (make two):
With smallest needles, CO 185 sts. K one row. BO.
Weave in ends.

FINISHING

Steam-block legwarmers flat. Using turning ridges
as a guide, turn under and press both top and
bottom 4 rows. Mattress St seams tog (see page 25),
beg at bottom, being careful not to pull tightly to
ensure an invisible seam. Stop seaming 2" from top.
Fold top edge to WS and sew into place, leaving
sides open for cord. Hem bottoms as for top. Attach
a big safety pin to one end of cord and pull through
casing. Remove pin. Tie into bows and get fabulous!

knit wit

Keep a notebook devoted to your knitting.
A blank sketchbook or unlined journal is ideal.
For each project, attach a length of the yarn
and the yarn label. Add photos and sketches
of the project as it progresses. Whenever
you're feeling uninspired, you can go
back and look at the progress
you've made.

rockstar scarf

**DESIGNED BY JILLIAN MORENO
FOR ACME KNITTING COMPANY**

Tell someone you're knitting a scarf and you might get an "oh, that's nice, dear."
But show them this butt-kicking scarf and they'll beg you to make them one.

Don't you love having power like that?

This design combines two so-good-you-want-to-eat-them yarns:
hand-painted Koigu merino and Apart, a super-silky faux fur.
The garter stitch construction is easy,
but learning to work with fuzzy
yarn takes a little patience.
The result? Strangers will
pet you when you wear
this scarf. Just ignore 'em—
you're a rockstar.

FINISHED MEASUREMENTS

Width: 6"

Length: 66"

MATERIALS

(MC) Koigu Premium Painter's Palette Merino (100% merino wool; 176yd/162m per 50g); color: P611X; 2 skeins

(CC) GGH Apart (100% nylon; 120yd/110m per 50g); color: 18; 1 skein

1 set US #3/3.25 mm straight needles

Yarn needle

GAUGE

24 sts/48 rows = 4" in garter stitch with MC

PATTERN

With CC, CO 35 sts. Work even in garter st for 6 rows.

Change to MC and work in garter st for 18 rows.

Continue working, alternating yarns as established, until work measures 66" from beg, ending with 6 rows of CC.

BO all sts.

FINISHING

Weave in ends and rock.

knit wit

If you drop a stitch while knitting with fuzzy yarn, it's easier to rip back and start over with that section of yarn than to try to find the dropped stitch.

free-standing muffler

DESIGNED BY MEGAN REARDON

Here's the perfect no-
fuss winter warmer: the
free-standing muffler. Sick
of scarves that whipped with
the wind or blew off altogether,
the designer wanted something
sleek and warm to fill the gap at her collar.
This muffler goes one better: instead of pulling it
over your head, making your hair all static-y and screwing up your lipstick, you simply
wrap it around your neck and secure it with hidden buttons before slipping on your coat.
IT'S AN IDEAL BEGINNING PROJECT. You take luscious angora/wool-blend
yarn, shape it simply, and you get simple perfection...something you made yourself that's
both functional and beautiful.

SIZE

S[M, L]

FINISHED MEASUREMENTS

Width: 17[18, 20]"
Length: 6"

MATERIALS

Tahki Imports Jolie (70% French angora, 30% merino wool;
108yd/100m per 25g); color: 5012; 2 skeins

1 set US #11/8 mm straight needles
Yarn needle
Two ball-shaped buttons, 0.5" diameter

GAUGE

12 sts/17 rows = 4" in St st with 2 strands held tog

Difficulty: 0 2

knit wit
33

STITCH PATTERN

2X2 RIB:

RS: K3, *p2, k2* rep from * to last st, k1.

WS: P3, *k2, p2* rep from * to last st, p1.

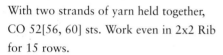

PATTERN

With two strands of yarn held together, CO 52[56, 60] sts. Work even in 2x2 Rib for 15 rows.

Row 16: P3 *kfb, k1, p2* to last st, p1. (64[69, 74] sts)

Row 17 and following odd rows: Work sts as they appear (p the p sts, k the k sts).

Row 18: P3 *k1, kfb, k1, p2* to last st, p1. (76[82, 88] sts)

Row 20: P3 *k1, kfb, k2, p2* to last st, p1. (88[95, 102] sts)

Row 22: P3 *k1, kfb, k3 p2* to last st, p1. (100[108, 116] sts)

Row 24: P3 *k1, kfb, k4, p2* to last st, p1. (112[121, 130] sts)

Row 25: Work sts as they appear. BO all sts in rib.

FINISHING

On the WS, attach the buttons at the edge, 1" in from top and bottom.

knit wit

Casting on and binding off with a needle a size or two larger than your working needle is an easy way to add stretch to an edge.

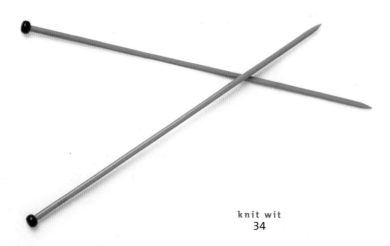

coif

DESIGNED BY MEGAN REARDON

Yes, hat head is bad, but what about ponytail head? That's when you'd really like to wear your hair back, but none of your hats are cooperating, and you're just not going to do a baseball cap today. It doesn't go with your heels.

Problem solved. The coif is a historically inspired design (think medieval nightcap) with updated color and style. A pretty headcovering that ties underneath your chin and covers your ears, it leaves the back of your head free for your hair to do what it needs. Quickly knit from cord to cord, it's a simple design with sweet results.

If your head (or hair!) is a little bigger than average, instructions for lengthening the coif are provided in the pattern.

FINISHED MEASUREMENTS

17.5" plus ties

MATERIALS

Rowan Cork (95% merino, 5% nylon; 120yd/110m per 50g); color: 048; 1 skein

1 set US #9/5.5 mm straight or circular needles
1 set US #10.5/7 mm straight or circular needles
Yarn needle

GAUGE

14.5 sts/21 rows = 4" in St st on larger needles

Difficulty: 02

CORD:

With smaller needles, CO 2 sts. Work even in St st for 11", ending with RS facing.

HAT:

Change to larger needles.

Row 1: K1, m1, k1.

Row 2 and all WS rows: P.

Row 3: K3.

Row 5: K1, m1, k1, m1, k1.

Row 7: K2, m1, k1, m1, k2.

Row 9: K2, m1, k3, m1, k2.

Row 11: K2, m1, k5, m1, k2.

Row 13: P3, m1, k5, m1, p3.

Row 15: K4, m1, k5, m1, k4.

Row 17: P3, k2, m1, k5, m1, k2, p3.

Row 19: K.

Row 21: P3, k3, m1, k5, m1, k3, p3.

Row 23: K.

Row 25: P3, k4, m1, k5, m1, k4, p3.

Row 27: K.

Row 29: P3, k5, m1, k5, m1, k5, p3. (23 sts)

Row 31: K.

Row 33: P3, k17, p3.

Row 35: K.

Row 36: P.

Rep rows 33–36 7 times.

To lengthen coif, rep rows 33–36. Each additional rep will inc the finished length by approx 1".

Row 65: P3, k5, k2tog, k4, k2tog, k4, p3.

Row 67: K.

Row 69: P3, k4, k2tog, k4, k2tog, k3, p3.

Row 71: K.

Row 73: P3, k3, k2tog, k4, k2tog, k2, p3.

Row 75: K.

Row 77: P3, k2, k2tog, k4, k2tog, k1, p3.

Row 79: K4, k2tog, k4, k2tog, k3.

Row 81: P3, k2tog, k3, k2tog, p3.

Row 83: K2, k2tog, k4, k2tog, k1.

Row 85: K1, k2tog, k3, k2tog, k1.

Row 87: K1, k2tog, k1, k2tog, k1.

Row 89: K1, k2tog, k2tog.

Row 91: K3.

Row 93: K1, k2tog.

CORD:

Change to smaller needles. Work even in St st for 11". BO.

Weave ends into cords.

knit wit

Knit a sampler of various increases and decreases using leftover yarn. You will be able to see how the stitches look in your own knitting and determine which increase will look best. Refer to the sampler later when you need to remember what the stitches should look like.

pixie hat

DESIGNED BY SARAH MUNDY

Sometimes a toque is just wrong, a beret is too fiddly, and your hood bores you. You need a pixie.

Barely more difficult to make than a scarf, this charming design is surprisingly versatile. The optional fuzzy trim is worked with a double-knitting technique, so that the right side is a layer of eyelash yarn in reverse stockinette stitch and the wrong side is a layer of smooth yarn in seed stitch. Don't be scared of this…it's actually quite fun and you absolutely can do it.

CAVEAT: wear your pixie and be prepared to make friends with strangers in the supermarket.

Difficulty: 01 (sleek) 02 (furry)

SIZE

S[M, L, XL]

FINISHED MEASUREMENTS

Head circumference: 21[22, 23, 24]"

MATERIALS

(MC) Cascade 220 (100% wool; 220yd/200m per 100g); color: 9456 Blue; 1 skein

For furry version, add:
(CC) Pelsgarn Funny (100% polyester; 100yd/90m per 50g); color: 6355 Denim Blue; 1 skein

1 set US #7/4.5 mm straight needles

1 set US #8/5 mm straight needles

2 US #7/4.5 mm double-pointed needles

Stitch holder

Yarn needle

GAUGE

20 sts/24 rows = 4" in St st on larger needles

STITCH PATTERN

SEED ST:
All rows: *K1, p1* to last st, k1

PATTERN

TRIM:
You can choose to frame your face with fur—or not.
Follow directions for the trim option of your choice.

Option: Sleek
With MC and smaller needles, CO 73[77, 83, 87]
sts. Work even in Seed St until 1" from beg, ending
with RS facing.
Next row: Change to larger needles. K1[3, 6, 8],
(k11, inc 1) 5 times, k to end of row.

Option: Furry
*As you work, hold CC yarn on RS of work and MC
yarn on WS of work. Do not twist yarns together
between stitches.*
With smaller needles, holding MC and CC tog,
CO 73[77, 83, 87] sts.
Row 1: Using CC, p1 through the CC strand of
first st, holding yarn to RS. Using MC, k1 through
MC strand of first st, holding yarn to WS. *P1 CC,
p1 MC, p1 CC, k1 MC, rep from * to end of row.
Row 2: *K1 MC, k1 CC, p1 MC, k1 CC* to last
2 sts, k1 MC, k1 CC.
Rep Rows 1 and 2 twice more to make 6 rows of
trim. Break CC and secure end.
Next row: Change to larger needles. K2tog
(1 strand CC, 1 strand MC) 1[3, 6, 8] times,
(k2tog 11 times, k2) 5 times, k2tog to end of row.

MAIN HAT:
Beg with a WS row, work even in St st until work
measures 6[6.25, 6.5, 7]" from beg.

Shape back:
Dec 1 st at each edge on next 12[12, 14, 14] rows.
BO 8[9, 9, 9] sts at beg of next 4 rows. BO rem sts.

FINISHING

Press slightly to flatten, and fold in half with sides
together. Mattress st (see page 25) back seam.

BOTTOM TRIM:
With smaller needles, pick up and knit
59[61, 63, 67] sts around bottom edge of hat.
Work even in Seed St for 5 rows.
Next row: P3, place these 3 sts on a holder,
BO 53[55, 57, 61] sts, p3.

TIES:
With DPNs, I-cord (see page 25) the 3 rem sts for 9".
Break yarn and pull tail through sts. Using a
yarn needle, pull end of yarn to inside of I-cord.
Rep with 3 sts from holder.
Remove markers.
Weave in
ends.

knit wit

A knitting buddy is great for morale and
productivity! Chances are you already
know a knitter who would love to
meet every week or two for tea and
knitting. Hint: She (or he) might
not be your own age.

nosewarmer, 2nd generation

DESIGNED BY AMY R. SINGER

When my sister and I were little, Grandma knit for us. I loved her nosewarmers—tiny nose cones secured around the head with ties and decorated with a tassel. I have a vivid memory of the scent of frosty winter air coming through the warm fabric she'd knitted.

I recently tried to re-create her pattern and ended up with a mess. Giving up in frustration, I went back to knitting a sock. And as I finished the short-row toe, I realized I had a new kind of nosewarmer staring me in the face! A few adjustments, and poof! Second-generation nosewarmers were born.

My husband doesn't quite understand them, and believe me, I know they're silly. But when you're five years old and it's an icy winter day, it's fun to tie on one of these before heading out in the cold. Everyone else's nose freezes but yours.

Difficulty: 0 2

SIZE

Child[Adult]

MATERIALS

(MC) Cascade Fixation (98.3% cotton, 1.7% elastic; 100yd/92m [relaxed] per 50g); color: 6185 Hot Pink; 1 ball

(CC) Cascade Fixation; color: 9942 Variegated Pink; 1 ball

1 set US #2/2.75 mm straight or double-pointed needles

Sharp yarn needle

GAUGE

36 sts/56 rows = 4" in St st (unstretched)

PATTERN

NOSEWARMER:

With MC, CO 20[25] sts. P 1 row.

Begin shaping:

K to last st, wrap st, turn.

Next row: P to last st, wrap st, turn.

Cont as est, until 8[10] sts are wrapped on each side of needle and 4[5] live sts rem.

Next row: Work to first wrapped st. Work wrap and st tog. Turn. Rep last row until all 20[25] sts are live again. BO all sts.

FINISHING

Weave in ends.

TASSEL:

Create tassel by wrapping CC around 3 fingers 8–15 times. Carefully remove yarn from fingers and slide loops over a pencil or chopstick. Take a 12" length of CC and tie it around loops below stick. Wrap the yarn around and around until the tassel is held securely. Knot tightly and cut open bottom loops. Trim tassel to uniform length. Slide tassel off stick and sew to the front of nosewarmer using MC, going through the top loop of the tassel at least twice to secure it.

TIE:

With CC, create two braids 15[18]" long. With MC, secure one tie to the inside on each point of the nosewarmer.

knit wit

Learn to knit socks. Having a sock on the go at all times is the best thing for knitter's block, travel, or waiting. Socks are small projects you can take everywhere. They're mostly mindless knitting, which makes them great in-the-car projects on long trips (as long as you're not the driver). They're very good hand occupiers when the next step in a pattern is too much for your brain but your fingers aren't tired yet. Best of all, hand-knit socks make the recipient, even if it's only you, very happy.

sacred & profane convertibles

DESIGNED BY JILLIAN MORENO FOR ACME KNITTING COMPANY

Wristwarmers are great, but what happens when your fingers get chilly? These pop-top mittens are the ideal solution.

Knit in delicious Koigu Kersti variegateds, solids, or a combination of both, the mitten tops button on when you need them. And when you don't, pop them off and tuck them in your pocket for later. Big bonus points for getting to dip into your button stash!

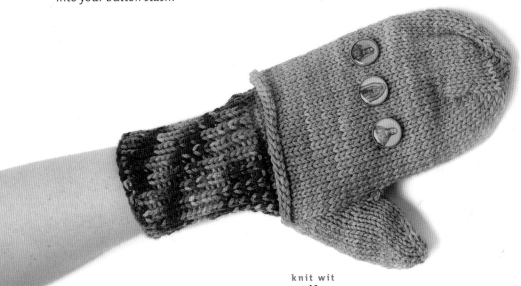

SIZE

Women's medium

FINISHED MEASUREMENTS

Wristwarmer:

Hand: 7.5" around

Length: 7.5"

Pop-top:

Hand: 8.5" around

Length: 7.75"

MATERIALS

(MC) Koigu Kersti (100% merino wool; 114yd/105m per 50g); color: K136; 1 skein

(CC) Koigu Kersti; color: K2130; 1 skein

1 set US #6/4 mm double-pointed needles

Stitch holder

Yarn needle

6 buttons, 0.5" diameter

STITCH PATTERN

1X1 RIB:

K1, p1, rep around

GAUGE

20 sts/30 rows = 4" in St st

PATTERN

WRISTWARMER (make two):

With MC, CO 38 sts. Div bet 3 needles: 12 sts, 14 sts, 12 sts. PM, join and work in k1, p1 rib for 3".

Thumb gusset:

**Rnd 1: K1, m1, work to last 2 sts, k1, m1, k1.

Rnd 2 and all even rnds: K.

Rnd 3: K2, m1, k to last 3 sts, k1, m1, k2.

Rnd 5: K3, m1, k to last 4 sts, k1, m1, k3.

Rnd 7: K4, m1, k to last 5 sts, k1, m1, k4.

Rnd 9: K5, m1, k to last 6 sts, k1, m1, k5.

Rnd 11: K6, m1, k to last 7 sts, k1, m1, k6.**

Rnd 12: K to last 7 sts. Slip next 14 sts on holder for thumb. Remove marker.

CO 2 sts on the RH needle. (38 sts) Work even in St st until piece measures 7.5" from beg, ending with RS facing. BO.

Thumb:

Div thumb sts from holder bet 3 needles. Pick up 2 sts from the hand where it meets the thumb. (16 sts) Work even in St st for 1", ending with RS facing. BO.

POP-TOPS:

With CC, CO 44 sts. Div bet 3 needles: 14 sts, 16 sts, 14 sts. P 1 rnd. K 1 rnd.

Thumb gusset:

As for wristwarmer from ** to **

Rnd 13: K7, m1, k to last 8 sts, k1, m1, k7.

Rnd 15: K8, m1, k to last 9 sts, k1, m1, k8.

Rnd 16: Work to last 9 sts. Sl next 18 sts to holder for thumb.

CO 2 sts on the RH needle. (44 sts) K 1 rnd. Sl 1 of the new sts to LH needle. K 2 rnds.

Left-hand buttonholes:

Rnd 1: K7, BO 2 sts, k3, BO 2 sts, k3, BO 2 sts, k to end of rnd.

Rnd 2: K7, CO 2 sts, k3, CO 2 sts, k3, CO 2 sts, k to end of rnd.

Right-hand buttonholes:

Rnd 1: K25, BO 2 sts, k3, BO 2 sts, k3, BO 2 sts, k to end of rnd.

Rnd 2: K25, CO 2 sts, k3, CO 2 sts, k3, CO 2 sts, k to end of rnd.

knit wit

Develop and maintain a large yarn stash and shop with an enabler. You'll always have yarn when you want to start something new at 2:00 a.m. And when you're broke, you can trade with your friends.

POP-TOPS (continued):

Work even in St st until piece measures 5.5" from beg.

Next rnd: *K9, k2tog* around.

Next rnd: *K8, k2tog* around.

Next rnd: *K7, k2tog* around. Cont decs as est until 8 sts rem. Break yarn and thread tail through rem sts. Pull tight to the inside and secure.

Thumb:

Div 18 thumb sts from holder bet 3 needles. Pick up 2 sts from the hand where it meets the thumb. (20 sts) Work even in St st for 1.5".

Begin decreasing: **Rnd 1:** *K3, k2tog* around.

Rnd 2: K.

Rnd 3: *K2, k2tog* around.

Rnd 4: K.

Rnd 5: *K1, k2tog* around. Break yarn and thread tail through rem sts. Pull tight to the inside and secure.

FINISHING

Weave in ends. Sew buttons on wristwarmers to correspond with pop-top buttonholes.

dreadlock hat

DESIGNED BY AMY SWENSON

Dreadlocks are very cool, but they're a long-term commitment not everyone wants to make. Wear this dreadlock hat when you need extra mojo; take it off when it's time to run a comb through your hair.

The dreads are constructed as I-cords of different lengths, sewn together and felted for dense fuzziness. Once felted, sew the dreads to the simple stockinette hat, and voila! Instant island style, no wax necessary! If dreads aren't your thing, just knit the hat and you have a fab fitted cap.

Difficulty: 0 3

SIZE

XS[S, M, L, XL] (child to adult)

FINISHED MEASUREMENTS

Hat circumference: 16[18, 20, 22, 24]"

MATERIALS

(MC) Lorna's Laces Bullfrogs and Butterflies (85% wool, 15% mohair; 190yd/175m per 4oz); color: Denim; 1 skein

(CC) Lorna's Laces Bullfrogs and Butterflies; color: Rainbow; 1 skein

1 set US #10/6 mm double-pointed needles
1 set US #8/5 mm double-pointed needles
Yarn needle

GAUGE

16 sts/22 rows = 4" in St st on smaller needles

PATTERN

HAT:

With MC and smaller needles, CO 64[72, 80, 88, 96] sts. PM and join. Work in the round, even in St st, until piece measures 5[5, 5.25, 5.5, 6, 6.25]" from beg with brim held flat.

Next rnd: *K2tog, k6* around. (56[63, 70, 77, 84] sts) Work 4 rnds even.

Next rnd: *K2tog, k5* around. (48[54, 60, 66, 72] sts) Work 3 rnds even.

Next rnd: *K2tog, k4* around. (40[45, 50, 55, 60] sts) Work 2 rnds even.

Next rnd: *K2tog, k3* around. (32[36, 40, 44, 48] sts) Work 1 rnd even.

Next rnd: *K2tog, k2* around. (24[27, 30, 33, 36] sts) Work 1 rnd even.

Next rnd: *K2tog, k1* around. (16[18, 20, 22, 24] sts)

Next rnd: K2tog around. (8[9, 10, 11, 12] sts) K2tog 4[4, 5, 5, 6] times, k0[1, 0, 1, 0].
(4[5, 5, 6, 6] sts)

Break yarn, leaving a long tail. Thread tail through rem sts with yarn needle. Pull tight but do not sew in end.

DREADS:

All dreads are worked on larger DPNs with CC.

Anchor dread:

CO 3 sts. Work I-cord (see page 25) for specified length for your size. K3tog and slide st to right end of needle. This is the center stitch of the anchor dread. (K1, p1, k1) into same st. Slide sts to right end of needle. Continue to work I-cord for specified length. Cut yarn and thread through sts. Pull tight and secure end.

Regular dread:

Find center st on anchor dread. Pick up and knit 1 st into this center st and slide active st to right end of needle. (K1, p1, k1) into same st. Slide 3 sts to right end of needle. Continue to work I-cord for specified length. Cut yarn and thread through sts. Pull tight and secure end.

FOR XS, S:

Base Dreads

Make 1 anchor dread 18" long. Make 7 regular dreads 9" long beg with center st of anchor.

Middle Dreads

Make 1 anchor dread 14" long. Make 7 regular dreads 7" long beg with center st of anchor.

Top Dreads

Make 1 anchor dread 10" long. Make 7 regular dreads 5" long beg with center st of anchor.

FOR M, L, XL:

Base Dreads

Make 1 anchor dread 24" long. Make 7 regular dreads 12" long beg with center st of anchor.

Middle Dreads

Make 1 anchor dread 18" long. Make 7 regular dreads 9" long beg with center st of anchor.

Top Dreads

Make 1 anchor dread 12" long. Make 7 regular dreads 6" long beg with center st of anchor.

FINISHING

Stack 3 sets of dreads so that center sts align. Use tail or waste yarn to firmly sew sets together. Tie remaining ends together or loosely sew into center of I-cords so dreads will not unravel while felting. Follow felting instructions on page 25. Dreads may tangle while felting. To prevent knots, check dreads every 5 minutes while in the washer and untangle as necessary. When the dreads are fully felted, run through a minute or two of the spin cycle, remove, and let air dry. Once dry, use the yarn tail from the hat to sew on the dreads. With scissors, trim off unwanted fuzz. Weave in rem ends.

knit wit

To select a suitable yarn for felting, choose 100 percent animal fiber, such as wool, mohair, or alpaca, and be sure it's non-superwash. Superwash wool is treated to survive the washing machine without shrinking. While this is great for sweaters, socks, and other frequently laundered garments, superwash wool will not felt at all.

third-eye chullo

DESIGNED BY MELISSA WALTERS

You may have seen a chullo hat. You may even have knitted one. But I doubt that yours has given you mystical powers.

This third-eye chullo will. It takes the magic number three to the extreme, incorporating three rings on the crown of the hat, three ridges to define the hat's body, and three-stitch I-cords. The embroidered third eye, a symbol dating back to ancient Babylon, is the final touch.

If you're a mom, freak out the kids by wearing the eye at the back of your head and make good on your reputation.

SIZE

One size fits most adults

FINISHED MEASUREMENTS

Circumference: 21"

Length (not including ear flaps)**:** 7.5"

MATERIALS

Version 1 (shown on page 47):

(MC) Manos Del Uruguay (100% wool; 138yd/126m per 100g); color: W Persimmon; 1 skein

(CC) Manos Del Uruguay; color: 111 Eclipse; 1 skein

Version 2 (shown below):

(MC) Manos Del Uruguay; color: 59 Kohl; 1 skein

(CC) Manos Del Uruguay; color: 04 Turquoise; 1 skein

1 set US #8/5 mm double-pointed needles

1 16" US #8/5 mm circular needle

Stitch markers

Sharp yarn needle

GAUGE

17 sts/22 rows = 4" in St st

STITCH PATTERN

SPLIT-CHAIN ST:

Using the eye graphic below as a guide, determine eye motif position by marking the boundaries with spare yarn. Thread yarn needle with an 18" length of contrasting yarn. Bring the threaded needle from the back of the knitted fabric to the front and make a stitch that is approx 0.25" long. With the next st, bring the needle up from the back in the center of that first st to split the yarn. Each new st splits the prev st.

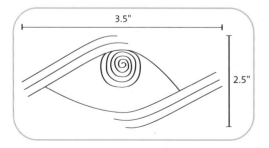

3.5"

2.5"

TOP:

With DPN and MC, CO 3 sts. Work in I-cord (see page 25) for 3".

CROWN:

Div sts onto DPNs so that there is 1 st on each needle.

Row 1: Kfb into each st. (6 sts) PM bet first and second st on first needle to identify beg of row.

Row 2 and all following even rows: K.

Row 3: K1, m1, *k2, m1* to last st, k1. (9 sts)

Row 5: *K1, m1*. (18 sts)

Row 7: *K2, m1*. (27 sts)

Row 9: *K3, m1*. (36 sts)

Row 11: *K4, m1*. (45 sts)

Row 13: Change to CC, *k5, m1*. (54 sts)

Row 15: Change to MC, *k6, m1*. (63 sts)

Row 17: Change to CC, *k7, m1*. (72 sts)

Row 19: Change to MC, *k8, m1*. (81 sts)

Row 21: Change to CC, *k9, m1*. (90 sts)

Row 23: Change to MC, k.

Change from DPNs to circ when you have enough sts to knit comfortably. PM before first st of round.

BODY:

K7, k2tog around. (80 sts)

Work even in garter st for 6 rounds.

K8, m1 around. (90 sts)

Work even in St st to 3" past inc round.

K7, k2tog around. (80 sts)

Work even in garter st for 6 rounds.

FIRST EAR FLAP:

BO 23 sts. With DPN, k 16. (17 sts on DPN) Leave remaining sts on circ. Work in garter st on only these 17 sts for 5 more rows.

Flap shaping:

Row 1: K6, ssk, k1, k2tog, k6.

Row 2 and all following even rows: K.

Row 5: K5, ssk, k1, k2tog, k5.

Row 7: K4, ssk, k1, k2tog, k4.

Cont dec as established, working 1 less st on each side of the decs every other row until 3 sts rem. Work in I-cord for 9". BO.

SECOND EAR FLAP:

With RS facing, join MC to the sts on circ. BO 23 sts. With rem 17 sts, complete second ear flap as first.

FINISHING

Weave in ends. Loosely knot I-cord at the top of the hat. Knot the bottom of the ear flap I-cords. Make eye motif using Split-Chain St. Because the thickness of Manos varies, you may need to add extra rows of stitching to fill in eye motif. Block if necessary.

knit wit

The SSK decrease is particularly pretty. Slip the first stitch knitwise onto RH needle, slip the second stitch purlwise onto RH needle. Insert LH needle into both stitches and k2tog.

fuzzy feet redux

DESIGNED BY THERESA VINSON STENERSEN

If you've taken a peek at what knitters are blogging* about on the Internet, you'll know felting is huge. Everyone's knitting wool things and shrinking them…on purpose! There's a good reason. Felting your own knits (see page 25) gives you custom results.

To make these super cozy felted slippers, you knit a pair of gigantic socks at a loose gauge. The felting process, which uses a household washing machine, makes the wool fabric thick, sturdy and lightweight—perfect for slippers!

This pattern comes in 12 sizes from teeny-weeny baby to big bad daddy and is ideal for customization. Add stripes, use variegated or tweed yarns, put fluff at the cuff. Since all yarns behave differently during the felting process, knit and felt a test swatch before you knit the real things.

blog = weblog: a web page with pictures, text, and links to other websites of interest.

MATERIALS

Child: Cascade 220 (100% wool, 220 yd/200m per 100g); color: 7802 Cerise; 1 skein

Adult: Cascade 220; color: 9547 Cobalt; 2 skeins

Scrap novelty yarn for cuff (optional)

1 set US #10/6 mm double-pointed needles
1 16" US #10/6 mm circular needle (optional)
Yarn needle

GAUGE (pre-felting):

14 sts/20 rows = 4" in St st

SIZES

Child: 0–2[2–4, 4–6, 6–8, 8–10, 10–12] years
Adult: XS[S, M, L, XL, XXL]

FINISHED MEASUREMENTS

Slipper length after felting:
Child: 5.5[6.5, 7.5, 8.5, 9, 9.5]"
Adult: 10[10.5, 11, 11.5, 12]"

STITCH PATTERN

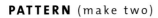

SL 1:

RS: hold yarn to back and slip knitwise.
WS: hold yarn to front and slip purlwise.

PATTERN (make two)

Child: Use DPNs.
Adult: Work cuff and foot in the round on circ. Use DPNs for heel and toe decreases on all sizes once there are too few sts to fit around circ.

CUFF:

CO 28[32, 32, 36, 36, 40], 40[44, 48, 52, 56, 56] sts very loosely.
Div sts evenly bet needles, join and PM. Work even in St st for 2.5".

HEEL FLAP:

At beg of next rnd, k 7[8, 8, 9, 9, 10], 10[11, 12, 13, 14, 14] sts, turn.

Sl 1, p 14[16, 16, 18, 18, 20], 20[22, 24, 26, 28, 28], turn.

Ignoring rem sts on the needles which will become the instep, work the heel flap flat in St st as follows:
Row 1: Sl 1, k 14[16, 16, 18, 18, 20], 20[22, 24, 26, 28, 28], turn.
Row 2: Sl 1, p 14[16, 16, 18, 18, 20], 20[22, 24, 26, 28, 28], turn.
Repeat these 2 rows 7[8, 8, 9, 9, 10], 10[11, 12, 13, 14, 14] more times or until the heel flap is approx as long as it is wide.

Turn heel:
Continuing on heel sts only:
Row 1: K 9[10, 10, 11, 11, 12], 12[13, 14, 15, 16, 16], k2tog, k1, turn.
Row 2: P 6, p2tog, p1, turn.
Row 3: K to last st before gap created by last turn, k2tog [1 st from each side of gap], k1, turn.
Row 4: P to last st before gap created by last turn, p2tog [1 st from each side of gap] p1, turn.
Repeat Rows 3 and 4 until no sts rem on either side of gap, ending with RS facing.

Gusset shaping:

K to center of heel sts, PM to indicate beg of rnd, k remaining heel sts. Pick up and knit 8[9, 9, 10, 10, 11], 11[12, 13, 14, 15, 15] sts through the elongated Vs along the left edge of heel flap, PM (Marker 1), k across sts held for instep, PM (Marker 2), then pick up and knit 8[9, 9, 10, 10, 11], 11[12, 13, 14, 15, 15] sts through the elongated Vs from the right edge of heel flap and complete rnd. Work heel and instep tog in the rnd from this point.

Rnd 1: K, sl markers as you come to them.
Rnd 2: K to 2 sts before Marker 1, k2tog, sl marker, k to Marker 2, sl marker, ssk, complete rnd.

Rep these two rnds until 28[32, 32, 36, 36, 40], 40[42, 44, 46, 48, 48] sts rem.

FOOT:

Child: Leave markers in place.
Adult: Remove side markers, but leave the marker indicating the beg of rnd.

Work even in St st until work measures 6[8, 10, 11, 12, 13], 13[13.5, 14.5, 15, 16, 17]" in length from back of heel.

Decrease for toe:

Adult: Place markers for toe dec as follows: k 10[10, 11, 11, 12, 12], PM (Marker 1), k 20[21, 22, 23, 24, 24], PM (Marker 2), complete rnd.
All sizes:
Rnd 1: *K to 3 sts before Marker 1, ssk, k1, sl marker, k1, k2tog, rep from * for second marker.
Rnd 2: K.
Rep these two rnds until 8[12, 12, 16, 16, 20], 16[18, 20, 14, 16, 16] sts rem.

Div sts evenly at the markers onto two needles with the sts from top of sock on one needle and sts from bottom on the other. Break yarn leaving 12" tail and close toe using Kitchener st or 3-needle BO (see page 25). Loosely weave in any ends using yarn needle.

FINISHING

Follow felting instructions on page 25. *Instead of using machine*, rinse by hand to remove soap residue, then machine spin to remove as much water as possible. Pull and tug on the slippers to adjust for length, then either form to shape by stuffing with plastic bags or put them on your feet over another pair of socks and let air dry for a perfect fit. For children or for use on slippery floors, attach a non-skid sole.

When your fuzzy feet get dirty, wash with care as for any other hand-knit item; slippers will continue to felt and shrink if subjected to hot water, soap, and agitation.

knit wit

To avoid a tight, inflexible cast-on edge, use the simplest cast on of all: cast on by knitting on. Place a slip knot on your LH needle (making sure that the loop gets tighter when you pull on the tail end rather than the yarn attached to the ball) and knit into the knot as if it were a regular stitch.

Transfer the new stitch to the LH needle and repeat the process until you have as many stitches as you need.

your
arms
are full

**DON'T CARRY YOUR PRECIOUS
STUFF AROUND IN UGLINESS.**
Plastic grocery bags are meant
to hold spinach and chocolate chip cookies,
not your knitting-in-progress
or your music device of choice.
And they certainly aren't suitable
for your new laptop!
Knit something fabulous.
Large selection within, no waiting.

ice cream pint cozy ✳ laptop sampler ✳ sound-system snugglers
suki II tote ✳ serenity yoga mat bag ✳ water-bottle sling

ice cream pint cozy

DESIGNED BY ERICA HOHMANN

Believe it or not, the average North American considers a pint of ice cream one serving. Hmm.

Even if you're not that hungry, you certainly don't want your fingers freezing as you indulge. Now they won't. Just knit this pretty cozy, slip it over a pint of mocha-choka-la-ga-yaya, and dig in. When you're done (a serving or a pint…we won't judge), slide off the cover and save it for next time.

FINISHED MEASUREMENTS

Top circumference: 10.5"

Bottom circumference: 7"

Height: 3.75"

MATERIALS

Cascade Fixation (98.3% cotton, 1.7% elastic; 100yd/92m [relaxed] per 50g); color: 9936; 1 ball

1 set US #7/4.5 mm double-pointed needles

Yarn needle

GAUGE

24 sts/40 rows = 4" in St st

Difficulty: 0 1

STITCH PATTERN

2X2 RIB:
K2, P2, rep from * to beg of round.

PATTERN

CO 64 sts. Div sts evenly over needles. Join, being careful not to twist. Work in 2x2 Rib for 6 rows then work even in St st until piece measures 1.25" from beg.

Next rnd: (K14, k2tog) 4 times.
Work even until piece measures 2.5" from beg.

Next rnd: (K13, k2tog) 4 times. (42 sts)
Work even until piece measures 3.75" from beg.

Shape bottom of pint:
Next rnd: (K4, k2tog) 8 times.
Work 1 row even.
Next rnd: (K3, k2tog) 8 times.
Work 1 row even. Cont dec as est, working every other row even and working 1 st fewer between decs until 8 sts rem. Break yarn, leaving a long tail. Thread tail through rem sts with yarn needle. Pull tight and secure.

FINISHING

Weave in ends. To block, thoroughly clean an empty ice cream pint inside and out. Dampen cozy with lukewarm water and stretch over ice cream pint until edge is lined up evenly under lip of pint. Allow cozy to dry.

knit wit

When you get a new pair of circular needles, they're coiled up pretty tightly. To straighten out the coils into one gentle loop, fill up a large bowl with very hot (not boiling!) water and soak the coil section for a few minutes. Then hang the needle over a doorknob, or through the handle on the refrigerator door until the needle cools down.

laptop
sampler

DESIGNED BY IVETE TECEDOR

Just blown big piles of cash on a laptop? The last
thing you want are stupid scratches on its shiny
new surface. This laptop sampler does two
things at once: it protects your baby from
poky things and it lets you play with
different stitch patterns.

Simple combinations of
knit and purl stitches create
texture and look mighty
fine. Knit the small
version for a
12-inch iBook
or the large
one for your
average laptop.
And pick funky
buttons to close
the flap…just
because you can.

Difficulty: 0 2

SIZE

S[L]

FINISHED MEASUREMENTS

Length: 12[13]"
Width: 9[11]"
Depth: 1[1.5]"

MATERIALS

Cascade 220 (100% wool; 220yd/201m per 100g);
color: 9404 Red; 2 skeins

1 24" US #5/3.75 mm circular needle
1 24" US #6/4 mm circular needle
Three buttons, $7/8$" diameter
2 stitch markers
Yarn needle

GAUGE

21 sts/27 rows = 4" in St st on larger needle

STITCH PATTERNS

1X1 RIB (FLAT):
RS: *K1, p1,* rep to end
WS: *P1, k1,* rep to end

1X1 RIB (ROUND):
K1, p1 around

SEED ST:
Rnd 1: *K1, p1* around
Rnd 2: *P1, k1* around

BOX ST:
Rnds 1–2: *K2, p2* around
Rnds 3–4: *P2, k2* around

DOUBLE SEED ST:
Rnds 1–2: *K1, p1* around
Rnds 3–4: *P1, k1* around

PATTERN

FLAP:

With smaller needles, CO 60[66] sts.
Work back and forth in 1x1 Rib for 1".

BUTTONHOLES:

Next row: Cont in 1x1 Rib, work 8[9] sts,
BO 4 sts, (work 16[18] sts, BO 4 sts) 2 times,
work 8[9] sts.
Next row: Cont in 1x1 Rib, work 8[9] sts,
CO 4 sts, (work 16[18] sts, CO 4 sts) 2 times,
work last 8[9] sts.
Cont even in 1x1 Rib until flap measures 3.5[4]".

BODY:

CO 68[74] sts at beg of row. (128[140] sts)
PM and join. Working in the rnd, cont in 1x1 Rib
for 1[1.5]".
Change to larger needle. K to last 2[3] sts, PM,
k to next marker, remove last marker (marker
shows the new beg of each rnd).
Work Seed st for 2[2.5]".
Work 7 rnds in garter st.
Work Box st for 2[2.5]".
Work 7 rnds in garter st.
Work Double Seed st for 2[2.5]".

BOTTOM:

Work 9 rnds in garter st. Turn work inside out and
BO using 3-needle BO (see page 25).

FINISHING

Weave in ends. Block to measurements.
Attach buttons to correspond with buttonholes.

knit wit

Measure gauge over different areas of your
item as you knit. Your gauge can change
drastically from start to finish depending
on your mood or surroundings.

sound-system snugglers

DESIGNED BY STEFANIE JAPEL

Is it anyone's business what portable music player you listen to? I think not! The perfect camouflage are these sound-system snugglers that keep your cool tunes warm and private. **AND YOU HAVE TO LOVE THIS:** they transform your headphones into stylish earmuffs!

SIZE

Portable cassette player-sized
[Portable compact disc player-sized]

FINISHED MEASUREMENTS

Player covers: 4 x 6.25"[6.25 x 6.25"]

Earphone covers: 3" in diameter

MATERIALS

(MC) Schachenmayr Nomotta Brazilia/Salsa bi-color (100% polyester; 97yd/90m per 50g); color: 235 Purple [269 Blue]; 1 skein makes both sets

(CC) Schachenmayr Nomotta Bravo (100% polyacryl; 162yd/150m per 50g); color: Black; 1 skein makes both sets

1 set US #9/5.5 mm needles

Yarn needle

Button

Difficulty: 0 2

GAUGE

16 sts/18 rows = 4" in St st with one strand of each yarn held tog

Next row: K2, YO, k2.
Next row: Skp, k1, k2tog. (3 sts)
Next row: K3tog, cut yarn and pull the tail through last st to secure yarn.

FINISHING

HEADPHONE SNUGGLERS:
Using yarn needle and tail of yarn, work in running st around the edge of each earpiece cover. Pull yarn tail to gather really tightly. Secure covers to headphone earpieces by tying loose yarn to the earphone headband.

PLAYER SNUGGLERS:
Fold rectangular piece in half up to the button flap and mattress stitch up each side. Weave in ends. Sew on button to correspond with buttonhole. Insert musical device and crank it.

PATTERN

HEADPHONE SNUGGLERS (make two):
Holding one strand of each yarn tog, CO 6 sts.
Row 1, 3 & 5 (WS): P.
Row 2, 4 & 6: M1, k to last st, m1. (12 sts)
Work even in St st until work measures 2" from beg, ending with RS facing.
Skp, k to last st, k2tog on next and every other row 2 times. (6 sts)
BO all sts, break yarn leaving an 8" long tail.

CASSETTE/CD PLAYER SNUGGLER:
Holding one strand of each yarn tog, CO 26 sts.
Work even in St st until piece measures 8[12.5]" from beg, ending with RS facing.

Button flap:
Next row (RS): Skp, k to last st, k2tog.
Next row: K.
Repeat these 2 rows 10 times. (4 sts)
Work in garter st for 3 rows.

knit wit

When teaching others to knit, I encourage them to keep their first projects. It's fun to look back on the first cast-on row and the first dropped stitches. It will record your progress as your stitches become more even and fewer are dropped...all the way through to your first bind off.

suki II tote

DESIGNED BY KATHY WORTEL

The shaping of this fun felted bag
is simple, and the personal touch
comes from what you do with the
pattern…You can make it solid or
striped; add fuzz at the edge or not;
make it taller by knitting a longer
tube. You have total control.
EXTRA COOL FEATURE:
when changing colors, just tie a square
knot to attach the new color and trim
the ends of the knot to one inch on the
inside of the bag. The ratty ends
will conveniently felt when washed,
securing them permanently, and you'll
never see them again. Love that.

FINISHED MEASUREMENTS (after felting)

Height: 13"

Width: 10"

MATERIALS

(MC) Cascade 220 (100% wool, 220yd/200m
per 100g); color: 7816; 2 skeins

(CC1) Cascade 220; color: 7809; 2 skeins

(CC2) Cascade 220; color: 7810; 2 skeins

(CC3) Schachenmayr Salsa (100% polyester,
65yd/60m per 50g); color: 70; 1 ball

1 set US #11/8 mm double-pointed needles

1 32" US #11/8 mm circular needle

Yarn needle

Sewing needle

Complementary sewing thread

GAUGE (before felting)

11 sts/16 rows = 4" in St st with 2 strands of MC held tog

Difficulty: 0 2

STITCH PATTERN

STRIPE SEQUENCE:
CC1: 8 rnds. **MC:** 3 rnds. **CC2:** 8 rnds.
MC: 3 rnds. **CC1:** 8 rnds.

DIRECTIONS

Yarn is used doubled throughout.

TOTE BAG:
Using double strand of MC, CO 112 sts with circ.
Join and k one rnd. With 1 strand MC and 1 strand
CC3, k 8 rnds. Break CC3.
Work in Stripe Sequence until there are 4 stripes of
CC1 and 3 stripes of CC2.
Next rnd: With MC, k2tog, k54, k2tog, k54.
K next 2 rnds.

Shape bottom:
Cont with MC, switching to DPNs as needed.
Rnd 1: *K9, k2tog* around.
Rnd 2 and all even-numbered rnds: K.
Rnd 3: *K8, k2tog* around.
Cont dec as est, working 1 st fewer between
decs every odd-numbered rnd until 20 sts rem.
Next rnd: *K2tog, rep from * around. (10 sts)

FINISHING

Break yarn, leaving a long tail. Thread tail through
rem sts with yarn needle. Pull tight. If there is a
small hole in the center, stitch over it a few times to
close. Weave in end.

HANDLES (make two):
With a single strand of CC1 and circ, CO 120.
Do not join. Work 10 rows in garter st. BO all sts.

FELTING

Follow felting instructions on page 25. Immediately
after removing from spin cycle, pull bag into desired
shape and flatten any creases. Stuff the bag with
rolled towels to block, or lay flat on a clean surface,
and allow to dry. The bag's handles will be slightly
curved or twisted when first removed from washing
machine. Use your fingers to pull them flat, pinning
down the ends with heavy objects to keep them flat
as they dry. When dry, sew handles to inside of bag.

knit wit

Swatching is essential for all felting projects
because certain colors felt more quickly than
others. Some light-colored yarns have been
bleached prior to dyeing, which can make
them difficult to felt. If you want to use
a light-colored yarn, knit a swatch
first and test felt it.

serenity yoga mat bag

DESIGNED BY STEPHANNIE ROY

Knitting and yoga go very well together, but your yoga teacher might not be too impressed to see you casting on when everyone else is doing the downward dog. Instead, get your mat to class in this superfine knitted yoga bag.

This gorgeous and practical mat bag is made from delicious, washable Mission Falls 1824 cotton. It's knit in the round and has a sturdy-but-beautiful linen stitch strap. Knitting this bag in a tighter-than-normal gauge makes the bag stable and strong. If you want to choose your own colors, you will need roughly 600 yards total—100 yards for the strap, 100 yards for the top and bottom, and 400 yards for the body of the bag. Your bag should be about 1 inch longer than the width of your mat so it will still fit once the cotton has shrunk a smidge in the wash.

SIZE

To fit a standard yoga mat
24" wide x 68.5" long x $^3/_{16}$" thick
(superthick mats will likely fit too).

FINISHED MEASUREMENTS

Length: 30"

Circumference: 14.5"

Strap: 30"

MATERIALS

(MC) Mission Falls 1824 Cotton (100% cotton;
84yd/77m per 50g); color: 305 Lemongrass; 3 balls

(CC1) Mission Falls 1824 Cotton; color: 303 Jade; 2 balls

(CC2) Mission Falls 1824 Cotton; color: 103 Pebble; 1 ball

(CC3) Mission Falls 1824 Cotton; color: 207 Chili; 1 ball

(CC4) Mission Falls 1824 Cotton; color: 204 Lentil; 1 ball

(CC5) Mission Falls 1824 Cotton; color: 302 Wintergreen;
1 ball

(CC6) Mission Falls 1824 Cotton; color: 401 Chicory; 1 ball

(CC7) Mission Falls 1824 Cotton; color: 405 Phlox; 1 ball

(CC8) Mission Falls 1824 Cotton; color: 105 Graphite; 1 ball

(CC9) Mission Falls 1824 Cotton; color: 100 Ebony; 1 ball

1 set US #4/3.5 mm double-pointed needles

1 16" US #4/3.5 mm circular needle

1 US size E/3.5 mm crochet hook

Spring toggle closure

Stitch markers

Yarn needle

GAUGE

21 sts/34 rows = 4" in St st

Difficulty: 02

STITCH PATTERNS

LINEN ST:

Row 1: Sl 1, *k1, sl 1 purlwise
WYIF* repeat to last st, k1.

Row 2: Sl 1, *p1, sl 1 purlwise
WYIB* repeat to last st, p1.

YO2:

Bring yarn forward between sts and wrap
yarn around needle 2 times before making
next st.

STRIPE PATT

(# denotes the number of rnds):
4 jade, 2 ebony, 2 graphite, 3 wintergreen,
3 phlox, 4 lentil, 3 chicory, 2 chili,
3 jade, 4 pebble, 3 phlox, 2 lemongrass,
2 wintergreen, 3 chili, 2 lentil, 5 jade,
3 graphite, 2 ebony, 2 chicory, 3 chili,
3 lemongrass, 2 jade, 3 lentil, 3 wintergreen, 3 pebble, 4 chicory, 3 phlox.

 ## PATTERN

BAG:

With MC, CO 76 sts. Join and PM.
K 6 rnds. P 1 rnd. K 4 rnds.

Eyelet rnd: *K5, k2tog, YO2, k2tog
tbl, k6, k2tog, YO2, k2tog tbl,* repeat
to end of row (8 eyelets made).

Next rnd: K 1 rnd, working YOs tbl.
K 4 rnds. P 1 rnd. PM on the first st to
mark strap placement. Work even in St st
following stripe patt until bag measures
25.5" from first stripe or desired length.

Bottom shaping:

Change to MC, k 1 rnd.

P 1 rnd, PM on the first stitch to mark strap placement. K 1 rnd.

Dec rnd: *K2, k2tog* to end of row. (57 sts)

K 3 rnds.

Dec rnd: *K1, k2tog* to end of row. (38 sts)

Change to DPNs and k 2 rnds.

Dec rnd: K2tog to end of row. (19 sts) K 2 rnds.

Dec rnd: K2tog to last st, k1. (10 sts) K 1 rnd.

Dec rnd: K2tog to last st. (5 sts)

Break yarn, leaving a long tail. Thread tail through rem sts with yarn needle. Pull tight to the inside and secure.

STRAP:

With MC, CO 16 sts. K 1 row. P 1 rnd.

Change to Linen St and work until strap measures 30" or desired length (the strap will stretch when mat is in bag). Set aside.

 **FINISHING**

ATTACH STRAP:

Top of bag:

Using a DPN, pick up 8 p st ridges to left of marker, pick up marked st, pick up 7 to right of marker. With WS facing, attach strap to these picked-up stitches using 3-needle BO (see page 25).

Bottom of bag:

Sew strap to purl ridges at the marker to correspond to top.

STRING CLOSURE:

Using MC, single crochet a chain 30" long and secure ends. Thread cord through eyelets so ends are opposite the strap. Thread both ends through the toggle and slip knot together.

Weave in all ends.

knit wit

When you're almost at the end of a ball of yarn and aren't sure if you'll have enough for the next two rows, divide what's left in half and put a slip knot at the midpoint. Work the next row. If you get to the knot before you're finished, start a new ball on the next row. If you don't get to the knot, repeat the process until you do. This works best for plain garter and stockinette stitches, since patterning and texture can consume different amounts of yarn on each row.

water-bottle sling

DESIGNED BY JAMIE COOK-JAQUES

Carrying a water bottle around is an annoying
necessity when it's sticky-hot outside. So don't carry
your bottle—wear it!

This design is a perfect blend of simplicity,
function, and looks. The sling holds most
personal-sized water bottles and has a little
pocket on the strap to hold credit cards, ID, and
a few bucks. Most brilliantly, the bag is knit in the
round, so the only sewing involved is weaving
the ends when you're done.

REMEMBER: A full water bottle will pull
the sling lower, so wear the strap across your
body for comfort. The sling will spring back when
the bottle's empty, so you can slip the strap over
your shoulder again.

FINISHED MEASUREMENTS

NOTE: *Both measurements are for the empty sling.*

Length: 23.5" including strap

Width: 4.5"

MATERIALS

Koigu PPPM (100% merino wool; 175yd/160m per 50g);
color: P611X; 2 skeins

1 set US #2/2.75 mm double-pointed needles

Yarn needle

Stitch holder

Stitch marker

Difficulty: 0 3

GAUGE

32 sts/44 rows = 4" in St st

STITCH PATTERN

RIB PATT:
P3, k6 around

PATTERN

BOTTOM:

CO 7 sts.

Row 1: K.

Rows 2–9: Inc 1 st at each end. (23 sts)

Row 10: K.

Row 11: Inc 1 st at each end. (25 sts)

Rows 12–14: K.

Row 15: Inc 1 st at each end. (27 sts)

Rows 16–25: K.

Row 26: Dec 1 st at each end. (25 sts)

Rows 27–29: K.

Row 30: Dec 1 st at each end. (23 sts)

Row 31: K.

Rows 32–39: Dec 1 st at each end. (7 sts)
BO all sts.

BODY:

Pick up 81 sts around outside of circle. Div sts evenly on needles and work in the rnd even in St st for 2".

P 1 rnd. K 2 rnds. P 1 rnd. Work even in rib patt until piece measures 7" from bottom.

Next round: BO 21 sts purlwise, p15 sts, place these sts on a holder, BO 21 sts purlwise, p24. Cont working these 24 sts only, back and forth, for strap.

STRAP:

Row 1 (WS): P.

Row 2: K. Cont even in garter st for 4.25" *or* make optional pocket as follows:

OPTIONAL POCKET:

Rows 1–3: K.

Row 4: K3, *k1, m1* to last 3 sts, k3. (42 sts)

Row 5: K1, sl 1 purlwise WYIB, k1,* sl 1 purlwise WYIF, k1* to last 3 sts, sl 1 purlwise WYIB, k1, sl 1 purlwise. Repeat Row 5 for 3.75" from beg of pocket.

Next row: K3, *sl 1 to holder, k1* to last 3 sts, k3 (24 sts on needle, 18 sts on holder).

Cont STRAP (both versions):

Next row: K11, k2tog, k11.

Next row: K9, k2tog, PM, k1, PM, k2tog, k9. Working in garter st, k2tog before the first marker and after the second marker every 4" 3 times. (15 sts) Cont even in garter st until work measures 32" from beg of strap.

FINISHING

STRAP:

Being careful not to twist strap, bring right sides of strap tog and attach to holder sts on WS using 3-needle BO (see page 25).

POCKET:

Transfer sts from holder to needle; rejoin yarn on RS and BO all sts purlwise.

Weave in ends.

knit wit

Don't be afraid of anything. If you know how to knit and purl, and increase and decrease, you have the basics to conquer any pattern, learning as you go. Take classes, keep a journal, and take pictures of everything you make. Let your creativity guide and inspire you. And knit with the best yarn you can afford.

you
knit
that?

IF IT'S FLEXIBLE, YOU CAN KNIT WITH IT.
Almost everything you wear that isn't woven
is knit (unless you wear lots of rubber,
and that's none of my business).
Your jersey t-shirt is knitting, but teensy.
Scale it up and you can start to see
all sorts of materials in a new way.
And wait till you see what you end up with.
A knitted cowgirl belt?
A ballet-tulle scarf? You bet.

jelly scarf (or belt) ✳ corral belt ✳ birdless boa ✳ darci scarf
surf & turf skirt ✳ girly boxers

jelly scarf (or belt)

DESIGNED BY LESLIE PETROVSKI

As a kid at camp, I spent hours braiding gimp (maybe you called it lanyard or boondoggle) into yards and yards of skinny, square uselessness. We all did.

A little more practical, yet still nostalgic, this scarf is created from that same plastic lacing, as an homage to the squishy jelly shoes of the eighties. It's translucent and gelatinous and can transform a ho-hum outfit into an ensemble of haute kitsch.

Gimp assumes a jewelry-like aspect when knit tightly, but becomes more like fabric when knit loosely. Play with the stuff. Experiment with different stitches and needle sizes. Embellish with fringe, beads, or plastic toys. Wear it as a belt! Now that's *almost* useful.

Difficulty: 01

FINISHED MEASUREMENTS

Width: 4.25"

Length: 55"

MATERIALS

Rexlace® craft lacing (plastic vinyl; 100yd/90m per spool); color: Clear Raspberry; 1 spool (available at hobby and craft stores)

1 set US #13/9 mm straight or circular needles

1 blow dryer

1 butane lighter

GAUGE

11 sts/18 rows = 4" in garter stitch

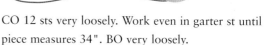

PATTERN

CO 12 sts very loosely. Work even in garter st until piece measures 34". BO very loosely.

FINISHING

Weave in ends. To secure your raw ends, lightly melt them with a butane lighter. While the plastic is still soft and hot, press it to the rest of your piece so the melted end binds to the rest of your scarf. Don't burn yourself!

To block, stretch your scarf to finished measurements and pin to a rug or carpet. Set your blow dryer on high, and blow it till it stays flat. Allow to cool. Unpin and enjoy.

knit wit

Begin to "free range" knit as soon as you can, altering designs to suit your body, breaking away from patterns entirely when you're ready. Free your knitting and your mind will follow. (And unless you have a cast-iron stomach, never knit through a turbulent descent on an aircraft.)

corral belt

DESIGNED BY REBECCA HATCHER

Belts can be a big pain. The holes aren't always where you need them to be, and where you need them to be can change daily. Alfredo for dinner last night and tiramisu for dessert? Ahem.

Braided belts are better, and now you can knit your own in leather. The $1/8$-inch-wide suede leather lacing is made in tons of colors, comes on 25-yard spools, and is widely available at craft shops or on the web. The final touch is a custom belt buckle, this one created by nicnorman.com. If vintage is more your thing, scavenge for something unique at a thrift store.

FINISHED MEASUREMENTS

Length: Add 6–10" to your waistband measurement to get your belt's finished length. A belt for low-rise pants needs to be longer than a belt that sits at your waist.

Width: 2"

MATERIALS

Tejas suede leather lace, ($^1/_8$" wide, 25yd/23m per spool); color: Dark Brown; 1 spool* (available at craft stores or leatherfactory.com)

* Each inch of belt requires approximately 22" of cord. For a belt longer than 38", you'll need two spools. Join end of cord on first spool to beginning of second by sewing, end to end, with matching thread.

1 set US #13/9 mm straight needles

Hook-closure buckle (custom buckle shown available at www.nicnorman.com)

Sewing needle

Heavy-duty sewing thread to match leather

Clear-drying craft glue

GAUGE

12 sts/8 rows = 4" in St st

Difficulty: 0 1

PATTERN

CO 6 sts. Sl the first st of each row purlwise, work in St st until belt reaches desired length plus 2". BO all sts.

FINISHING

Weave in ends along CO and BO edges for reinforcement. Secure ends unobtrusively by sewing them tightly to the last st in each row with sewing thread. Cut ends close to thread. Secure knots in thread with tiny drops of glue. To attach buckle, slip one end of belt through ring on back of buckle. Fold belt at ring and sew in place. There's no need to sew through the leather: sew around the stitches, as when sewing knitted fabric, and secure knots with glue. The buckle's hook will fit into any stitch on the opposite end of the belt.

knit wit

When knitting with leather, try not to get obsessed with keeping it flat. The twists and contrasting edge color add texture and interest. The same goes for many ribbon yarns.

birdless boa

DESIGNED BY

MARIE-CHRISTINE MAHE

This animal-friendly, feather-free boa
is perfect for wild parties and photo
shoots on the Riviera.

It's based on an original woven technique by Helen Pope
that the designer learned from Susie Hodge. Wear your
birdless boa and feel good knowing no birds are running
around naked just because you needed a little glam.

FINISHED MEASUREMENTS

Length: 70"

MATERIALS

(MC) Ashford Tekapo (100% wool; 218yd/201m per 100g);
color: 22 Pumpkin; 1 ball

(CC1) Crystal Palace Iceland (100% wool; 110yd/100m
per 100g); color: 22 Pumpkin; 1 ball

(CC2) Crystal Palace Deco-Ribbon (70% nylon, 30% acrylic;
80yd/74m per 50g); color: 125 Tangerine/Lime; 1 ball

(CC3) Crystal Palace Tingle (100% polyester; 45yd/41m
per 50g); color: 3866 Sunset; 2 balls

1 set US #4/3.5 mm double-pointed needles

Difficulty: 0 2

GAUGE

20 sts/24 rows = 4" in St st with MC

STITCH PATTERNS

I-CORD:

Work 3 sts. Push these sts to the beg of the needle they're now on. Then, without turning the work, k the same sts again in the same order, pulling the yarn tightly behind the work. Repeat. Keep the first st of every "row" extra tight, as you'll be bringing the yarn across the back of the whole thing, forming a tube. With a bit of tugging, if necessary, the resulting object will look perfectly seamless.

CATCH CC:

Hold a piece of CC yarn at front of work and bring the MC yarn across it as you p the next st. Do not p the CC yarn, but rather catch it so both ends hang on the RS. This forms the feathery part of the boa.

PATTERN

With DPNs and MC, CO 3 sts.
Work in I-cord patt as follows:
Row 1: P1, Catch CC1, k2.
Row 2: K1, p1, Catch CC1, k1.
Row 3: K2, p1, Catch CC1.
Row 4: K3.
Rep these 4 rows to create body of boa. *At the same time*, add a length of CC2 or CC3 randomly in each row using Catch CC. For a natural-looking boa, go for controlled chaos over an ordered placement of the decorative yarns. When boa measures 70" long, BO all sts.

FINISHING

To even out the tension and make sure the bits are secured, gently pull the finished boa lengthwise in sections so that it relaxes to its full length.

knit wit

Read Elizabeth Zimmermann's *Knitting Without Tears*. It will help liberate you from patterns. It will also teach you how to knit loosely in continental style, enabling you to knit a lot faster and more efficiently, and spare your hands in the process.

darci scarf

DESIGNED BY CATHERINE SHU

Sometimes, you just need to be a ballerina.

Knit from soft tulle cut into strips, this simply elegant garter drop-stitch scarf is named in honor of Darci Kistler of the New York City Ballet. Darci was, at 16, the youngest principal in the NYCB's history and is currently its last principal dancer to have been trained by the great George Balanchine. The Darci scarf is evocative of the Sugarplum Fairy, one of the many Balanchine roles that she shines in.

FINISHED MEASUREMENTS

Length: 60" plus fringe

MATERIALS

6 yards of 72" wide pink tulle (buy the softest kind available)

3 yards of 0.5" pink satin ribbon

3 yards of 0.5" pale pink seam binding

1 set US #15/10 mm straight needles

1 US K/10.5 mm crochet hook

GAUGE

12 sts/16 rows = 4" in St st

Difficulty: 0 2

PREPARATION

Cut your tulle into 2" wide strips: roll tulle lengthwise into a long burrito and snip off 2" wide sections with a pair of sharp scissors. Take each strip of tulle and tie it firmly to the next piece, leaving approximately 2" long tails. Save 42 unknotted strips, cut 12" long, for fringe.

STITCH PATTERN

YO3:

Bring yarn forward between sts and wrap yarn around needle 3 times before making next st. On the following row, drop the extra wraps and gently pull down on the work to stretch out these sts.

PATTERN

With the tulle, CO 21 sts.
Work 12 rows in garter st.
Next row: *K1, YO3, rep from * to last st, k1.
Next row: K across, dropping the extra wraps from YO3s. (21 sts)
Repeat Rows 1–14 until work measures 60" from beg, ending with 12 rows of garter st. BO.

FINISHING

Trim the ends of tulle scattered throughout your scarf to 1" long. Cut the satin ribbon and seam binding into foot-long pieces. Take the 42 strips of tulle you have put aside and loop a piece of tulle into every st at either end of your scarf and secure, interspersing pieces of ribbon and seam binding throughout the fringe for added texture. Your scarf won't need blocking, but if your tulle came starched, gently rinse it and hang to dry.

knit wit

The best way to transport a working ball of yarn is in a flat-bottomed double-drawstring bag. The bottom allows the ball to either sit (if it's a center-pull ball) or roll around evenly. The double drawstring lets you hang the bag from your wrist as you knit. It works much better than plastic zipper bags, "yarn bras," or the bottom of your purse.

surf & turf skirt

DESIGNED BY KRISTI PORTER

The sassiest skirt ever is concocted out of a tube of knitted grass and the waistband from a pair of vintage surfer shorts. If you're not the grassy type, change the colorways to dark browns and earth tones and you'll have a faux fur mini. Just add a shimmery tank top and go dancing.

But if you knit it as shown, be prepared: surfer dudes will find it hard to keep their hands off your grass!

Difficulty: 0 2

FINISHED MEASUREMENTS

You decide.

The skirt shown measures 34" at the hip; the knitted portion is 10" long.

MATERIALS

(MC) GGH Vamos (100% polyamid; 80m per 50g); color: 11 Grass

To figure out your yarn requirements, multiply the hip measurement of your shorts by the length of skirt you desire (measured from the hip). Divide this result by 120. This will give you the number of skeins of Vamos you will need.

(CC) A few yards of unfurry yarn
it need not match the Vamos; it won't show

1 pair of surfer shorts from your closet or thrift store

1 24" US #5/3.75mm circular needle

Needle and thread

GAUGE

15 sts/18 rows = 4" in St st

This skirt is knit at a smaller gauge than the yarn's ball band suggests.

PREPARATION

SCORE SOME SHORTS:

Find a pair of surfer shorts. Choose a pair that fit well at the waist. Avoid zippers, but elastic waist, drawstring, buttons, or a velcro closure are fine. You're going to have to get the shorts on with the fly only half open since you will be cutting off the rest!

Put the shorts on and make a mark about an inch below your hip on each side. Cut the shorts off to this length. Turn under the bottom 0.5" and sew in place. If there is a fly, sew it together at the bottom. Leave velcro or buttons above the seam in place. Remove anything that gets in the way of sewing your skirt closed.

PATTERN

KNIT SOME GRASS:

Measure the circumference of your skirt at the bottom edge. Multiply this measurement by 3.75—your gauge per inch.

With MC and circ, CO the resulting number of sts. Join and work even in St st until the piece measures 10" or desired length. Try on the waistband and the grass tube to see if you like the length. You'll only lose a row or two in length when attaching the two pieces. Change to CC and BO all sts.

FINISHING

Turn the waistband and the skirt inside out and place the BO edge of the skirt just over the hemmed bottom of the waistband. You want the fabric portion to be on the *outside* of the skirt. They should overlap roughly 0.25". Pin together in several places, stretching the skirt evenly around the circumference. Using an overcast stitch, sew through each BO st and the underturned hem of the skirt about 0.25" from the edge. After you have sewn the two pieces together, break off thread and secure it. Turn the skirt right-side out. Sew through the waistband and the skirt very close to the edge of the waistband using a running stitch. Weave in any remaining ends of yarn and hit the beach!

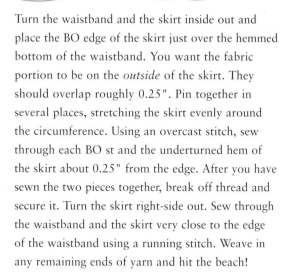

knit wit

If you've got some wool yarn in shades that leave you yawning, try dyeing them with Kool-Aid. For cotton yarns, tie-dye using boxed fabric dyes from grocery or craft stores.

girly boxers

DESIGNED BY NATALIE WILSON

The first rule of fight club is that the girl with the cutest boxer shorts has the advantage.

These are *cute*, and the ultimate in comfort. Treat your tush to these shorts in a dreamy soft cotton-tencel blend. The tapered shape ensures a flattering fit, and the button fly really works. The waistband, cleverly worked in stretchy cotton/elastic yarn, can be worn up or folded down, depending on how much belly you want to show.

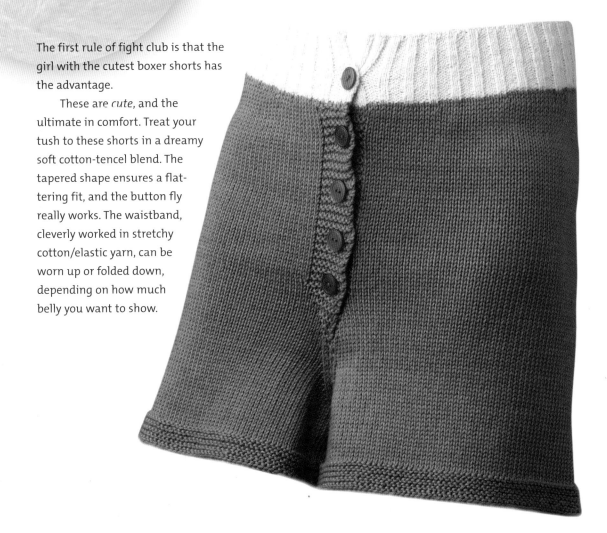

Difficulty: 0 4

SIZE

XS[S, M, L, XL, XXL]

FINISHED MEASUREMENTS

Hip: 35[38, 41, 44, 48, 52]"

Inseam: 2.5[2.75, 3, 3.5, 4, 4.5]"

MATERIALS

(MC) Cascade Yarns Pima Tencel
(50% pima cotton, 50% tencel;
109yd per 50g); color: 0499 silver;
5[6, 6, 7, 8, 10] skeins

(CC) Cascade Yarns Fixation
(98.3% cotton, 1.7% elastic;
100yd per 50g); color: 3077
pink lemonade; 1[1, 1, 1, 2, 2] balls

1 32" US #5/3.75mm circular needle

1 32" US #4/3.5mm circular needle

Row counter

Stitch holders

Yarn needle

Split ring markers

5 buttons, 0.75" diameter

Sewing needle and thread

GAUGE

22 sts/28 rows = 4" in St st using
US #5/3.75mm needle

STITCH PATTERNS

SSK: With yarn in back, sl 2 sts sep as if to k.
K these 2 sts tog tbl.

SSP: With yarn in front, sl 2 sts sep as if to k.
P these 2 sts tog tbl.

Single dec at beg of RS rows:
Work over first 4 sts – k2, ssk.

Single dec at end of RS rows:
Work over last 4 sts – k2tog, k2.

Single dec at beg of WS rows:
Work over first 4 sts – p2, p2tog.

Single dec at end of WS rows:
Work over last 4 sts – ssp, p2.

PATTERN

LEFT SIDE

Note: *On RS rows, center back is on RH side
(beg of row), center front is on LH side (end of row).*
With MC and US #4/3.5mm needle,
CO 138[150, 160, 170, 187, 204] sts. K 9 rows.
Change to US #5/3.75 mm needle. Beg with a
k row (RS), work in St st until piece measures
2.5[2.75, 3, 3.5, 4, 4.5]" from beg, ending with
RS facing.

Shape crotch curve:

Row 1 (RS): BO 3[4, 6, 8, 14, 19] sts, k to end.
Row 2: BO 3[3, 4, 4, 4, 10] sts, p to end.
Row 3: BO 6[8, 8, 9, 4, 7] sts, k to end.
Row 4: BO 3[2, 2, 3, 4, 1] sts, p to end.
Row 5: BO 3[2, 3, 1, 3, 3] sts, k to end.
Row 6: BO 1[1, 1, 2, 2, 2] sts p to end.
(119[130, 136, 143, 156, 162] sts)

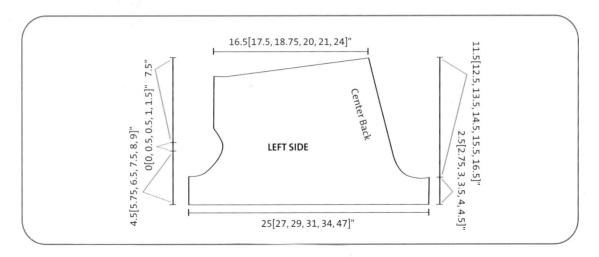

16.5[17.5, 18.75, 20, 21, 24]"

11.5[12.5, 13.5, 14.5, 15.5, 16.5]"

7.5"

0[0, 0.5, 0.5, 1, 1.5]"

4.5[5.75, 6.5, 7.5, 8, 9]"

2.5[2.75, 3, 3.5, 4, 4.5]"

Center Back

LEFT SIDE

25[27, 29, 31, 34, 47]"

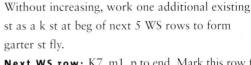

Cont shaping:

Dec 1 st at each edge every row 7[5, 0, 5, 7, 0] times, then every other row 0[5, 9, 3, 3, 8] times, then every 4th row 0[0, 0, 2, 2, 2] times.

Work 1 WS row even after last dec row.

(105[110, 118, 123, 132, 142] sts)

At center back edge, dec 1 st on next row, then every 6th row 0[0, 0, 5, 0, 8] times, then every 4th row 12[12, 13, 6, 15, 0] times. *At the same time,* when work measures 4.5[5.75, 7, 8, 9, 10.5]" from beg, at beg of next WS row, k1, m1, p to end.

Without increasing, work one additional existing st as a k st at beg of next 5 WS rows to form garter st fly.

Next WS row: K7, m1, p to end. Mark this row for placement of lowest button. Cont even, working 8 k sts for garter st fly at beg of WS rows, until piece measures 12[13.25, 14.5, 15.75, 16.5, 18]" from beg, ending with RS facing. (94[99, 106, 113, 119, 135] sts)

Shape waistline using short rows:

Row 1: Dec 1[1, 1, 0, 0, 0] st at beg of row, k to last 8 sts, wrap and turn.

Row 2 and all WS rows: P 1 row even.

Row 3: Dec 0[0, 0, 1, 0, 0] st at beg of row, k to last 19[21, 22, 21, 19, 20] sts, wrap and turn.

Row 5: Dec 0[0, 0, 0, 1, 1] st at beg of row, k to last 31[33, 35, 33, 30, 33] sts, wrap and turn.

Row 7: Dec 1[1, 1, 0, 0, 0] st at beg of row, k to last 43[46, 49, 41, 45] sts, wrap and turn.

Row 9: Dec 0[0, 0, 1, 0, 0] st at beg of row, k to last 55[58, 62, 59, 62, 58] sts, wrap and turn.

Row 11: Dec 0[0, 0, 0, 1, 1] st at beg of row, k to last 67[71, 76, 71, 63, 70] sts, wrap and turn.

Row 13: Dec 1[1, 1, 0, 0, 0] st at beg of row, k to last 79[83, 89, 84, 73, 82] sts, wrap and turn.

FOR SIZES L, XL, AND XXL ONLY:
Row 15: Dec 1[0, 0] st at beg of row, k to last 97[84, 95] sts, wrap and turn.

FOR SIZES XL AND XXL ONLY:
Row 17: Dec 1[1] st at beg of row, k to last 95[107] sts, wrap and turn.
Row 19: K 10[12] sts, wrap and turn.

FOR ALL SIZES:
P 1 row even. BO 1 st at center back, k to end picking up all wraps. (90[95, 102, 109, 115, 131] sts) Mark positions for 4 buttons centered on garter st fly, with the lowest at row marked during fly shaping, the uppermost 1" below top of piece, and rem 2 spaced evenly between. Sl sts to holder.

RIGHT SIDE

On RS rows, center front is on RH side (beg of row), center back is on LH side (end of row). Work as for left side, reversing all shaping. Work buttonholes on RS rows to correspond with marked positions using k4, yo, k2tog, cont in patt to end of row.

FINISHING

Sew left side and right side together at center back and at center front below fly. Sew inside leg seam.

WAISTBAND:
With RS facing, using CC and US #4/3.5 mm needle, k all sts from holder for left side, then k all sts from holder for right side. (180[190, 204, 218, 230, 262] sts) Work back and forth in k2, p2 rib for 7 rows.
Next row (RS): Rib 4, yo, k2tog, patt to end. Work even in ribbing for 15 more rows.
BO in rib (RS).
Sew on buttons to correspond with buttonholes. With right side lapped over left side, tack fly together through all layers below lowest button.

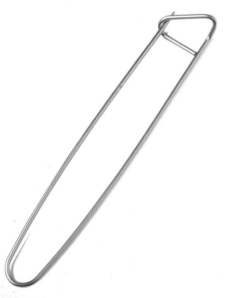

knit wit

Did you put your knitting down in the middle of a row and you're confused about where to start up again? The last stitch worked is the one with the yarn trailing out of it. The needle with that stitch on it goes in the hand where your work accumulates—the right hand for most knitters.

you've got nothing to wear

ARE YOU CRAVING A NEW CARDIGAN?
A kicky skirt? A hoodie? Don't shop; knit!
Be your own tiny custom clothing factory.
It's the polar opposite of the mall…
relaxing, productive, *and* you end up
with cool stuff to wear in exactly the
color and texture you wanted.
Be nice to yourself, though,
and make sure you have good lighting,
a comfortable place to sit,
and some tunes to keep you company.

freak vest ✳ magic skirt ✳ kyoto pullover ✳ banff turtleneck ✳ janda hoodie
hidden agenda sweater ✳ purple haze cardigan ✳ coral bikini

freak vest

DESIGNED BY VÉRONIK AVERY

There are times when absolutely
nothing will make you as happy as
wearing a really fuzzy vest. Freak
is the definition of instant
knitting gratification; if you're
motivated, you can finish
it in a weekend.

    This garter stitch
design is worked in a
furry wool yarn, and
features armholes
deep enough to wear
over a favorite jacket.
Dress it up and it's
glam; dress it down
and it's hippie. Thanks
to the clever design, the
body is knit in one piece
and the shoulders are
bound off together—no
sewing necessary. Resist the
temptation to use a different
yarn. This vest works best in
non-slippery GGH Lara; other
yarns will likely cause frustration.

PATTERN

BODY:

CO 110[122, 134, 146, 158] sts. Work even in garter st until piece measures 11[11.25, 11.75, 12, 12.5]" from beg.

Shape armholes:

K 27[29, 30, 32, 35], BO 4[6, 10, 12, 12], k 48[52, 54, 58, 64], BO 4[6, 10, 12, 12], k to end. (27[29, 30, 32, 35] sts rem for each front, 48[52, 54, 58, 64] sts rem for back) Place right front and back sts on holders.

LEFT FRONT:

Working in garter st, dec 1 st at armhole edge every other row 2[3, 3, 3, 4] times, then every 4th row 1[1, 1, 2, 3] time[s]. (24[25, 26, 27, 28] sts) Work even until piece measures 6.75[7.25, 7.75, 8.25, 8.75]" from beg of armhole shaping.

Shape neckline:

BO 9[10, 10, 11, 11] sts at beg of next RS row then BO 2 sts at beg of foll 2 RS rows. Work 2 rows even and place rem 11[11, 12, 12, 13] sts on holder.

BACK:

With RS facing, pick up held sts for back. Working in garter st, dec 1 st at each edge every other row 2[3, 3, 3, 4] times, then every 4th row 1[1, 1, 2, 3] time[s]. (42[44, 46, 48, 50] sts) Work even until piece measures 7[7.5, 8, 8.5, 9]" from beg of armhole shaping.

SIZE

XS[S, M, L, XL]

Difficulty: 0 2

FINISHED MEASUREMENTS

Chest: 36[40, 44, 48, 52]"
Length: 21.25[22.5, 23.5, 25, 26]"

MATERIALS

GGH Lara (90% wool/10% nylon; 60yd/55m per 50g); color: 9 Red; 6[7, 8, 9, 9] skeins

1 set US #10.5/6.5 mm straight needles
1 set US #10.5/6.5 mm double-pointed needles
Stitch holders
Yarn needle

GAUGE

12 sts/19 rows = 4" in garter stitch

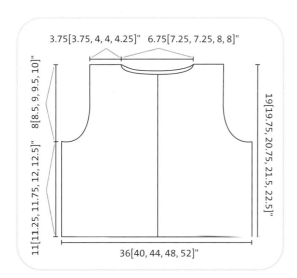

3.75[3.75, 4, 4, 4.25]"   6.75[7.25, 7.25, 8, 8]"

8[8.5, 9, 9.5, 10]"

11[11.25, 11.75, 12, 12.5]"

19[19.75, 20.75, 21.5, 22.5]"

36[40, 44, 48, 52]"

RIGHT FRONT:

Work as for left front, reversing all shapings.

FINISHING

Join Shoulders:

Place 11[11, 12, 12, 13] sts from left front shoulder and corresponding back shoulder on 2 DPNs and BO using 3-needle BO (see page 25). Rep with other shoulder. Sew in loose ends.

Shape neckline:

K 13[13, 14, 14, 15], place these sts on a holder. Join a second ball of yarn and BO 16[18, 18, 20, 20] sts, work to end. Work 1 row even.

Next row: BO 2 sts. (11[11, 12, 12, 13] sts) Work even until left side of back measures 8[8.5, 9, 9.5, 10]" from beg of armhole, ending with RS facing. Place sts on holder. With RS facing, join yarn and work across sts from holder.

Next row: BO 2 sts. (11[11, 12, 12, 13] sts) Work even until right side of back measures 8[8.5, 9, 9.5, 10]" from beg of armhole, ending with RS facing. Place sts on holder.

knit wit

Substituting novelty yarns can be a challenge, as every fiber behaves differently. But if you're allergic to wool and want to make this vest, you might have to try. Fiber content is key; no matter how much you want it to, a viscose yarn will not behave like a wool yarn. Swatching the potential replacement is of primary importance. Use a row counter and write down exact stitch and row counts. Block and measure the entire swatch. If your swatch is, say, 5.5 inches wide after blocking and has 20 stitches per row, divide 20 by 5.5. Your result, 3.63 in this case, is your number of stitches per inch. Multiply by 4 and you get 14.54 (round off to 14.5), and you have your gauge. Repeat for row gauge.

magic
skirt

DESIGNED BY KAT COYLE

If you can't bear hours of seaming when you're
done knitting, what you need are some projects
that are knit in the round. The magic skirt is an
easy in-the-round knit, with a flattering a-line
shape and a delicious textured border of
sequins and eyelash. To adjust the length of
the skirt to suit your particular legs, add or
subtract rounds between increases.

Inspiration came from the fun and
freedom of an old denim skirt the
designer made years ago, which she'd
adorned with vintage Mexican sequined
patches and feathers. The built-in glitz of
Berroco Plume FX and Mirror FX ensures that no
birds or showgirls were hurt in the making of this skirt.

SIZE

S[M, L, XL, XXL]

FINISHED MEASUREMENTS

Waist: 30[32, 34, 36, 38]"
Length: 24"

MATERIALS

(MC) Rowan Denim (100% cotton;
102yd/93m per 50g); color:
229 Memphis; 8[8, 9, 9, 10] skeins

(CC1) Berroco Mirror FX (100% polyester;
60yd/55m per 10g); color 9004
Silver/Black; 2[2, 3, 3, 4] skeins

(CC2) Berroco Plume FX Colors
(100% polyester; 63yd/58m per 20g);
color 6861 Blu-Dep; 2[2, 3, 3, 4] skeins

1 24" US #5/3.75 mm circular needle
1 29" US #6/4 mm circular needle
1 US F/3.5 mm crochet hook
Yarn needle
5 stitch markers

GAUGE

20 sts/28 rows = 4" in St st on larger needles

Difficulty: 0 2

STITCH PATTERNS

GARTER ST in the round:
K 1 rnd, p 1 rnd.

PICOT POINT BO:
BO 2 sts, *sl working st to LH needle, CO 2 sts.
BO 2 sts (completes one picot point), (k1, BO 1)
3 times*, rep from * to *.

PATTERN

WAISTBAND:
With MC and smaller needle, CO 148[160,
168, 180, 188] sts. PM and join.
Rnds 1 & 2: *K2, p2* around.
Rnd 3: *YO, k2tog, YO, p2tog* around.
Rnds 4 & 5: Rep Rnds 1 and 2.

BODY OF SKIRT:
Change to larger needle and work even in St st for 6 rnds.
Next row: K 37[40, 42, 45, 47], PM, m1, PM,
k 74[80, 84, 90, 94] PM, m1, PM, k 37[40, 42,
45, 47]. Work 6 rnds even in St st.
Next row: (K to first marker, m1, sl marker, k1,
sl marker, m1, k to third marker, m1, sl marker,
k1, sl marker, m1, k to end of row. Work 6 rnds
even in St st.) 18 times. (222[234, 242, 254, 262] sts)

BORDER:
Working in garter st (k 1 rnd, p 1 rnd), attach CC1
and work tog with MC.
*Work to first marker, m1, sl marker, work 1, slip
marker, m1, work to third marker, m1, sl marker,
work 1, sl marker, m1, work to end of rnd.
Work 6 rnds even.* Rep 2 times.

30[32, 34, 36, 38]"

24"

54[56, 58, 60, 62]"

Next round: Work to first marker, m1, sl marker, work 1, sl marker, m1, work to third marker, m1, sl marker, work 1, sl marker, m1, work to end of rnd. Work 3 rounds even. (234 [246, 254, 266, 274] sts) Break off CC1 and attach CC2 to work tog with MC. Work 3 rows even.

Next round: Work to first marker, m1, sl marker, work 1, sl marker, m1, work to third marker, m1, sl marker, work 1, sl marker, m1, work to end of row. Work 9 rounds even in garter st. (238[250, 258, 270, 278] sts).

BO using Picot Point BO.

FINISHING

Weave in ends. With MC, single crochet a tie 42[44, 46, 48, 50]" long. Lace it through the eyelets in waistband. Hand wash skirt in cool water, squeeze out excess water with a towel, and put through the spin cycle (only) of washing machine. Lay flat to dry.

knit wit

When using novelty yarns, take your time as you knit. The complexities of yarn texture make seeing stitches difficult and dropping stitches easy. Otherwise, go forward fearlessly!

kyoto pullover

DESIGNED BY KAREN STOCKTON

Kimonos are beautiful, but not exactly practical. This beautiful *and* wearable pullover was inspired by the Japanese summer-festival kimono, the yukata. It captures the yukata's vivid colors and features a bright built-in sash. Wear Kyoto on its own and show off your tum, or slip a contrasting, close-fitting tee underneath and let it peek out at the bottom. The knitting is simple. The finishing takes a little time, but it's so worth it.

SIZE

S[M, L, XL, XXL]

FINISHED MEASUREMENTS

Chest: 34[36, 38, 42, 44]"

Length: 19[19.5, 20.5, 22, 22.5]"

Upper Arm: 16[16.5, 17, 18, 19]"

MATERIALS

(MC) Tahki Cotton Classic [100% mercerized cotton; 108yd/100m per 50g]; color: 3703 Green; 8[8, 9, 10, 11] skeins

(CC1) Tahki Cotton Classic; color: 3454 Pink; 2[2, 3, 3, 3] skeins

(CC2) Tahki Cotton Classic; color: 3003 White; 1 skein

1 24" US #5/3.75 mm circular needle

Yarn needle

GAUGE

20 sts/27 rows = 4" in St st

STITCH PATTERN

DOUBLE SEED ST:

Rows 1 & 2: *k1, p1*, rep to end.

Rows 3 & 4: *p1, k1*, rep to end.

PATTERN

SASH:

With CC1, CO 170[180, 190, 210, 220] sts. PM and join. Work 1 row in Double Seed St. Change to CC2, work 2 rows in Double Seed St. Change to CC1, work even in Double Seed St until piece measures 5.5[5.5, 6, 6.5, 6.5]" from beg, ending with RS facing. Change to CC2, work 2 rows in Double Seed St. Change to CC1, BO.

BACK:

Work back and forth on circ.

With MC, CO 85[90, 95, 105, 110] sts. Work even in St st until piece measures 12[12.5, 13, 14, 14.5]" from beg, ending with RS facing.

Shoulder shaping:

BO 10[10, 11, 12, 13] sts at beg of next 6 rows.

BO rem 25[30, 30, 33, 32] sts.

LEFT FRONT:

CO 42[45, 47, 52, 55] sts with MC. Working in St st, dec 1 st at right edge every 6th row 0[15, 0, 8, 9] times then every 7th row 12[0, 14, 8, 8] times. (30[30, 33, 36, 38] sts)

Shoulder shaping:

Working in St st, BO 10[10, 11, 12, 13] sts at beg of next two WS rows. Work 1 row even. BO.

RIGHT FRONT:

Work the same as left front but reverse shaping, dec at the left edge, and BO the shoulder on RS rows.

SLEEVES:

With MC, CO 80[82, 84, 90, 95] sts. Work even in Double Seed St for 1.5". Work even in St st until 16[16.5, 17, 17.5, 18]" from beg. BO.

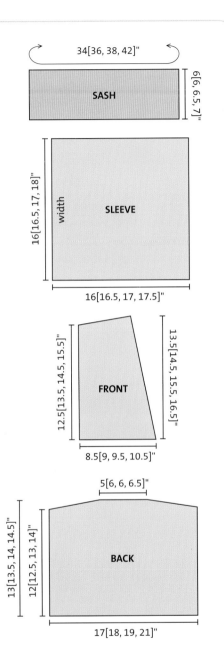

SASH

34[36, 38, 42]"

6[6, 6.5, 7]"

SLEEVE

width

16[16.5, 17, 18]"

16[16.5, 17, 17.5]"

FRONT

12.5[13.5, 14.5, 15.5]"

13.5[14.5, 15.5, 16.5]"

8.5[9, 9.5, 10.5]"

BACK

5[6, 6, 6.5]"

13[13.5, 14, 14.5]"

12[12.5, 13, 14]"

17[18, 19, 21]"

FINISHING

Block pieces to pattern measurements. Seam shoulders. Attach sleeves (center them against the entire side, end-to-end, not against the shoulder seam). Seam sleeves and sides.

Attach back to sash:

With CC1, stitch the top edge of the sash into the back of the CO edge of back.

Attach front to sash making sure that the front tips of left front and right front meet but don't overlap.

COLLAR:

With MC, CO 160[175, 185, 198, 206] sts. Working in Double Seed St, dec 1 st on each edge every 5th row 3 times. (154[169, 179, 192, 200] sts) Starting at the bottom right tip of left front, back-stitch the collar in place. Collar will finish tucked behind itself, left over right, at the point where collar/trim naturally crosses. Tack down both ends of collar and loosely secure all overlapping edges in front.

knit wit

Hand-knit fabric is stretchy, soft, and forgiving. Like most things in life, you can't force it, but you can urge it in the right direction.

banff turtleneck

DESIGNED BY JENNA WILSON

Think overstuffed armchair at a ski lodge with a cup of hot chocolate warming your hands, and you'll get why this yummy sweater is called Banff.

Nothing is comfier than this oversized pullover. Knit it in a durable, substantial tweedy yarn, and it will become your default sweater. It's a cinch to knit and the thoughtful design details, like the elegant raglans and shaped-sleeve ribbing (you can fold it back to create a slightly snugger cuff), will make you proud to tell people that you knit it.

Don't choose a wussy yarn for Banff. Pick something with body and you'll be rewarded with a sexy face-framing turtleneck.

SIZE

S–M[L–XL]

FINISHED MEASUREMENTS

Chest: 50[57]"

Length: 22[24]"

MATERIALS

Tahki Soho Bulky Tweed (100% wool; 110yd/100m per 100g); color: 304; 7[9] skeins

1 US #10/6 mm circular needle

Yarn needle

Stitch holders

GAUGE

14 sts/21 rows = 4" in St st

STITCH PATTERNS

2X2 RIB:

RS: *k2, p2* to last 2 sts, k2

WS: *p2, k2* to last 2 sts, p2.

RS DEC ROW:

K2, p1tbl, k2tog, work to last 3 sts, p1tbl, k2.

WS DEC ROW:

P2, k1tbl, p2tog tbl, work to last 3 sts, k1tbl, p2.

PATTERN

BACK:

CO 86[98] sts. Work in 2x2 Rib for 8".

Next row: Change to St st.

K19, m1, (k16[20], m1) 3 times, k19. (90[102] sts)

Work even for 13[19] more rows. BO 4[7] sts at beg of next 2 rows. (82[88] sts)**

Work RS Dec Row.

Work WS Dec Row.

Work these 2 rows a total of 24[27] times. (34 sts)

Right shoulder:

Row 1: K2, p1tbl, k2tog, k7, place rem sts on holder.

Row 2: P1, p2tog tbl, work to end.

Row 3: K2, p1tbl, k2tog, work to end.

Row 4: P1, p2tog tbl, work to end.

Work Rows 3 and 4 twice more. (4 sts)

Next row: K2tog, k2tog. Pass first st on RH needle over second st, break yarn, pull through rem st and secure.

Left shoulder:

With RS facing, join yarn at RH neck. BO center 10 sts. K1, k2tog, work to end.

Row 2: P2, k1tbl, p2tog tbl, work to end.

Row 3: K1, k2tog, work to end.

Row 4: P2, k1tbl, p2tog tbl, work to end.

Work Rows 3 and 4 twice more. (4 sts)

Next row: K2tog, k2tog. Pass first st on RH needle over second st, break yarn, pull through rem st and secure.

FRONT:

Work as for Back to **.

Work RS Dec Row.

Work WS Dec Row.

Work these 2 rows a total of 18[21] times. (46 sts)

Left shoulder:

Row 1: K2, p1tbl, k2tog, k14, place rem sts on holder.

Row 2: BO 2 sts, work to end.

Rows 3, 5, 7: K2, p1tbl, k2tog, work to end.

Rows 4, 6, 8: P1, p2tog tbl, work to end.

Row 9: K2, p1tbl, k2tog, work to end.

Row 10: Work even.

Rep Rows 9 and 10 five times more. (4 sts)

Next row: K2tog, k2tog. Pass first st on RH needle over second st, break yarn, pull through rem st and secure.

Right shoulder:

With RS facing, leaving center 8 sts of front on holder, join yarn after the last st on holder.

Row 1: BO 2 sts, work to end.

Row 2: P2, k1tbl, p2tog tbl, work to end.

Rows 3, 5, 7: K1, k2tog, work to end.

Rows 4, 6, 8: P2, k1tbl, p2tog tbl, work to end.

Row 9: Work even.

Row 10: P2, k1tbl, p2tog tbl, work to end.

Work Rows 9 and 10 five times more. (4 sts)

Next row: K2tog, k2tog. Pass first st on RH needle over second st, break yarn, pull through rem st and secure.

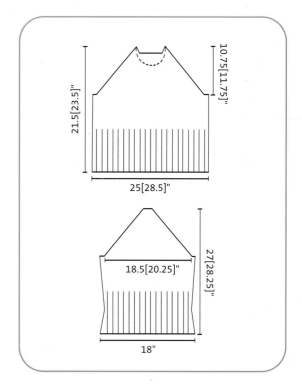

Sleeves (make two):

CO 66 sts. Work in 2x2 Rib for 16 rows.

Next RS row: K2, (p2tog, k2, p2, k2) 3 times, work to last 26 sts, (k2, p2, k2, p2tog tbl) 3 times, k2.

Next 7 rows: Work these 60 sts as they appear.

Next RS row: K2, (p1, k2, p2tog, k2) 3 times, work to last 23 sts, (k2, p2tog tbl, k2, p1) 3 times, k2.

Next 7 rows: Work these 54 sts as they appear.

Next RS row: K2, (p1, k2, m1, p1, k2) 3 times, work to last 20 sts, (k2, p1, m1, k2, p1) 3 times, k2.

Next 7 rows: Work these 60 sts as they appear.

Next row: K2, (m1, p1, k2, p2, k2) 3 times, work to last 23 sts, (k2, p2, k2, p1, m1) 3 times, k2.

Work 1 row even.

Next row: Change to St st and inc 4[8] sts evenly across row. (70[74] sts)

Work 43 rows more, inc 1 st at each side every 10th row 0[4] times. BO 4[7] sts at beg of next 2 rows. (62[68] sts)

Work RS Dec Row.

Work WS Dec Row.

Work these two rows a total of 27[30] times. (8 sts)

Next RS row: K2, p1tbl, k2tog, p1tbl, k2.

Next WS row: P2, k1tbl, k2tog tbl, p2.

BO rem 6 sts.

knit wit

The Banff turtleneck features a matched pair of decreases that create full-fashioned raglan shaping. Full fashioning means making your garment shaping a style detail, rather than hiding your increases and decreases in the seam allowances.

If you find the p2tog tbl tricky, here's how to handle it. Bring the yarn to the front of the work (since you're going to be purling). Insert the RH needle from L to R into the backs of the next two sts. The RH needle point will come forward naturally. Wrap from R to L and complete the stitch as if it were a single purl. It's fidgety, but it gets much easier as you get used to it. If your p2tog tbl stitch looks loose, give the working yarn a little extra tug to tighten it before continuing on with the rest of the row.

FINISHING

Block pieces. Mattress st (see page 25) raglan edges of sleeves to armhole edges of front and back, easing sleeves in if necessary. Mattress st underarm, sleeve, and side seams. Starting at seam along the neckline, pick up 4 sts along sleeve, 15 sts along side front neck, 8 sts along center front neck, 15 sts along side front neck, 4 sts along sleeve, 8 sts along side back neck, 10 sts along center back neck, and 8 sts along side back neck. (72 sts)

Join and mark beg of rnd. With RS facing, work in 2x2 Rib for 8 rnds.

Next rnd: (K2, p2tog, k2, p2) 9 times. (63 sts)

Next 5 rnds: Work sts as they appear.

Next rnd: (K2, p1, k2, p2tog) 9 times. (54 sts)

Next 9 rnds: Work sts as they appear.

BO in 2x2 Rib. Weave in loose ends.

ALAMEDA FREE LIBRARY

janda hoodie

DESIGNED BY AMY SWENSON

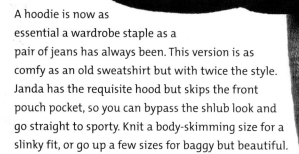

A hoodie is now as essential a wardrobe staple as a pair of jeans has always been. This version is as comfy as an old sweatshirt but with twice the style. Janda has the requisite hood but skips the front pouch pocket, so you can bypass the shlub look and go straight to sporty. Knit a body-skimming size for a slinky fit, or go up a few sizes for baggy but beautiful.

Difficulty: 0 4

SIZE

S[M, L, XL, XXL]

FINISHED MEASUREMENTS

Chest: 38[42, 46, 51, 55]"

Length: 21[21, 22, 23, 24]"

MATERIALS

(MC) Mission Falls 1824 Wool (100% wool; 84yd/77m per 50g); color: 028 Pistachio; 7[7, 8, 9, 10] skeins

(CC1) Mission Falls 1824 Wool; color: 022 Ink; 8[8, 9, 10, 11] skeins

(CC2) Mission Falls 1824 Wool; color: 001 Natural; 1 skein

1 US #6/4 mm circular needle

1 US #7/4.5 mm circular needle

1 US G/4 mm crochet hook

Stitch markers

Yarn needle

GAUGE

18 sts/24 rows = 4" in St st on larger needles

STITCH PATTERNS

SINGLE DEC ROW:
K1, ssk, work to last 3 sts, k2tog, k1.
(2 fewer sts on needle)

DOUBLE DEC ROW:
K1, ssk, ssk, work to last 5 sts, k2tog, k2tog, k1.
(4 fewer sts on needle)

3X2 RIB:
RS: *K3, P2, * rep across.
WS: *K2, P3, * rep across.

INSET RIB PATT:
RS: P2, k2, p2.
WS: K2, p2, k2.

CROCHET SL ST:
*Insert crochet hook under purl bump. Wrap yarn around hook once. Pull wrapped yarn under loop of MC and through loop of CC2. (If this is your first stitch, you will not have a loop of CC2.) You now have one loop of CC2 on hook. Repeat from *. Break yarn and pull tail through remaining loop.

PATTERN

BACK:
With MC and smaller needles, CO 85[95, 105, 115, 125] sts.
Work in 3x2 Rib for 2", ending with RS facing. Change to larger needles and work in St st until piece measures 12.5[12.5, 13, 13.5, 14]" from beg, ending with RS facing. BO 4[5, 7, 7, 9] sts at beg of next 2 rows. (77[85, 91, 101, 107] sts)

**Raglan Shaping:
Work Single Dec Row next, then every other row 22[16, 16, 17, 17] times. (31[51, 57, 65, 71] sts)
Work 1 row even.

M, L, XL, XXL SIZES ONLY—DEC AS FOLLOWS:
Row 1: Single Dec Row.
Row 2 & 4: P.
Row 3: Double Dec Row.
Repeat these 4 rows [2, 3, 4, 5] times more.
([33, 33, 35, 35] sts)

ALL SIZES:
Work Single Dec Row. (29[31, 31, 33, 33] sts)
Work 1 row even. BO.**

FRONT:

Work as for back. *At the same time,* when 43[51, 51, 51, 53, 53] sts rem on needle, P1 row, then begin shaping neck while continuing raglan dec as est. To shape neck, work first 21[25, 25, 26, 26] sts as est, attach second ball of MC, BO 1 st, work rem 21[25, 25, 26, 26] sts.

Dec 1 st each side of neckline on next and foll 8 rows, then work neckline even, continuing raglan dec as est.

SLEEVES (make two):

With CC1 and smaller needles, CO 45[50, 50, 55, 55] sts.

Work in 3x2 Rib for 2", ending with RS facing. Change to larger needles. K1, inc 1[0, 0, 1, 1] sts, work 18[21, 21, 23, 23] sts, PM, work Inset Rib Patt, PM, work 20[22, 22, 25, 25] sts. (46[50, 50, 56, 56] sts)

Work even, maintaining Inset Rib Patt, until piece measures 5" from beg.

Next row: *K2, m1, work as est to last 2 sts, m1, k2*.

Rep this row every foll 8[6, 6, 6, 4]th row 8[10, 15, 16, 21] times. (64[72, 82, 90, 100] sts) Work even until sleeve measures 18[19, 19.5, 19.5, 20]" from beg.

BO 4[5, 7, 7, 9] sts at beg of next 2 rows. (56[62, 68, 76, 82] sts)

Work as for back from ** to **. BO rem 8 sts.

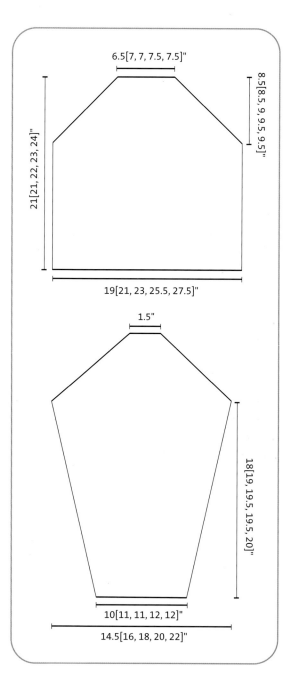

6.5[7, 7, 7.5, 7.5]"

8.5[8.5, 9, 9.5, 9.5]"

21[21, 22, 23, 24]"

19[21, 23, 25.5, 27.5]"

1.5"

18[19, 19.5, 19.5, 20]"

10[11, 11, 12, 12]"

14.5[16, 18, 20, 22]"

 **FINISHING**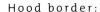

Block pieces to size and sew raglan seams.
Sew side and sleeve seams.

HOOD:

With CC1 and larger needles, pick up and knit
4[5, 5, 6, 6] sts across right front neckline, 8 sts
across right sleeve, 29[31, 31, 33, 33] sts along
back, 8 sts across left sleeve, 4[5, 5, 6, 6] sts along
left front neckline. (53[57, 57, 61, 61] sts)
Do not pick up sts inside V-neck. Turn.
K 19[21, 21, 23, 23], PM, k 15, PM, k19[21, 21,
23, 23].
Working in St st, inc 1 st before 1st marker and
after 2nd marker every other row 10 times.
(73[77, 77, 81, 81] sts)
Work even until hood is 9" long, ending with
RS facing.
K2tog after first marker and ssk before second
marker on next, then every foll 6th row twice,
then every foll 4th row twice, then every other
row 6 times. (51[55, 55, 59, 59] sts)
Work 1 row even. BO. Sew top hood seam.

Hood border:

With CC1 and larger needles, pick up and knit
15 sts along right V-neck edge, 130 sts along hood
edge, 15 sts along left V-neck edge. Do not join.
Turn and work in 3x2 Rib for 2", ending with RS
facing. BO in rib.

Sleeve stripes:

With CC2 and crochet hook, Crochet Sl St stripe
up center of each rev St st panel on sleeve, starting
at lower edge of sleeve. Each sleeve will have
two white stripes. Break yarn, pull tail through
remaining loop, and sew in ends.

knit wit

Instead of lugging around an entire book or
magazine, make *one* photocopy of the pattern
you're using. You can even enlarge those teeny
tiny charts, make notes, fold it up, and cross out
parts you've finished. It weighs nothing!
But only make copies of patterns you
own to respect copyright law.

hidden agenda sweater

**DESIGNED BY
KATE WATSON**

Sure, you knit this for him. Right. And whenever he leaves the house without it on, you wear it. Who could blame you?

It's handsomely knit in single-ply handspun, hand-dyed wool, and the saddle-shoulder construction is stylish and easier to do than it looks. A zipper lets you cool off or warm up, and a little pocket on the sleeve can hold an mp3 player or anything else that'll fit.

Difficulty: 0 4

SIZE

S[M, L, XL, XXL]

FINISHED MEASUREMENTS

Chest: 38[42, 46, 50, 54]"
Length: 27[28, 28, 29, 29]"

MATERIALS

(MC) Manos del Uruguay (100% wool; 138yd/126m per 100g); color: 55 Olive; 9[10, 11, 12, 13] skeins

(CC) Manos del Uruguay; color: 27 Petrol; 1 skein

1 24" US #10/6 mm circular needle
1 24" US #8/5 mm circular needle
1 6" closed-end zipper in coordinating color
Yarn needle
Split-ring stitch markers
Sewing thread and needle
Sturdy matching-colored yarn for seaming

GAUGE

16 sts/22 rows = 4" in St st on larger needle

STITCH PATTERN

2X2 RIB:

Row 1 (WS): *P2, k2,* rep from * to * to last 2 sts, p2.

Row 2 (RS): *K2, p2,* rep from * to * to last 2 sts, k2.

PATTERN

BACK:

**With CC, CO 86[94, 106, 114, 122] sts.

Work Row 1 (WS) of 2x2 Rib.

Next row: Change to MC, k 1 row.

Beg with a Row 2, cont even in 2x2 Rib until piece measures 16[16.5, 16.5, 17, 17]" from beg, ending with RS facing.

Shape armholes:

BO 4[4, 6, 6, 6] sts at beg of next 2 rows. Dec 1 st at both edges of next then every other row 3[3, 5, 5, 5] times. (70[78, 82, 90, 98] sts)**

Work even until piece measures 9.5[10, 10, 10.5, 10.5]" from beg of armhole, ending with RS facing. BO in 2x2 Rib. PM on last row 19[21, 23, 25, 29] sts in from each edge.

FRONT:

Work as for back from ** to **.

Work even until piece measures 5[5.5, 5.5, 6, 6]" from beg of arm-hole, ending with RS facing.

Shape neck:

Work across 34[38, 40, 44, 48] sts, place these on a holder, BO 2 sts. Work across 34[38, 40, 44, 48] sts.

RIGHT FRONT:

Work even in 2x2 Rib until piece measures 8[8.5, 8.5, 9, 9]" from beg of armhole, ending with RS facing.

***BO 8[10, 10, 11, 11] sts. Dec 1 st from neck edge each row 7[7, 7, 8, 8] times. (19[21, 23, 25, 29] sts)

Work even until piece measures 9.5[10, 10, 10.5, 10.5]" from beg of armhole, ending with RS facing. BO in 2x2 Rib.***

LEFT FRONT:

Sl the 34[38, 40, 44, 48] sts from holder to needle. With WS facing, join yarn and work even in 2x2 Rib until piece measures 8[8.5, 8.5, 9, 9]" from beg of armhole, ending with WS facing. Cont as for right front from *** to ***.

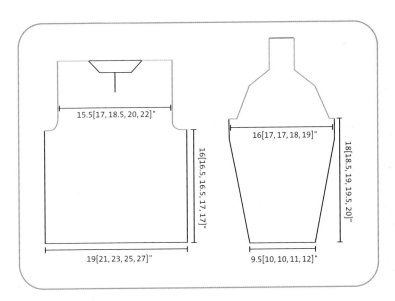

15.5[17, 18.5, 20, 22]"

16[16.5, 16.5, 17, 17]"

16[17, 17, 18, 19]"

18[18.5, 19, 19.5, 20]"

19[21, 23, 25, 27]"

9.5[10, 10, 11, 12]"

SLEEVES:

With CC, CO 42[46, 46, 50, 54] sts.
Work Row 1 (WS) of 2x2 Rib.
Next row: Change to MC, k 1 row.
Beg with a Row 2, work in 2x2 Rib, inc 1 st
at each edge on every foll 5th row 16 times to
74[78, 78, 82, 86] sts. Work even until piece
measures 18[18.5, 19, 19.5, 20]" from beg,
ending with RS facing.

Shape cap:

BO 4[4, 6, 6, 6] sts at beg of next 2 rows.
Dec 1 st at each side on next, then every other
row 13[11, 14, 16, 15] times, then every row
7[11, 6, 4, 7] times.
BO 2[2, 2, 3, 3] sts at beg of next 4 rows.

Saddle:

With rem 16 sts, cont even in 2x2 Rib (P1, [K2, P2]
to last st, P1) for 4 [4.5, 5, 5.5, 6.5]", ending with
RS facing. BO in 2x2 Rib.

POCKET:

With MC, CO 22 sts. Work in 2x2 Rib until pocket
measures 5.25", ending with RS facing. Change to
CC and k 1 row even. Work
Row 1 of 2x2 Rib.
BO in 2x2
Rib.

FINISHING

Block pieces to measurements. Mattress st pocket
(see page 25), placing CO edge 16" from beg of
sleeve-center pocket and line up ribs of pocket with
ribs of sleeve. To sew in sleeves, pin corner of saddle
flap to the back at marker. Continue to pin the
sleeve in so the opposite side of the flap meets up
with the shoulder BO of the front. The free end of
the saddle becomes part of the collar, to be picked
up later. Mattress st sleeves in place. Seam sleeves
and body.

COLLAR:

With smaller needle and RS facing, beg at right
front, pick up 22[26, 26, 30, 30] sts up to saddle,
14 sts from right saddle, 30[34, 34, 38, 38] sts from
back neck, 14 sts from left saddle, 22[26, 26, 30, 30]
sts down left front. (102[114, 114, 126, 126] sts)
Pay attention to how the collar's rib is placed when
you're picking up sts and skip picking up sweater sts
when necessary to line up ribs between sweater and
collar for a more professional appearance.
Beg with a WS row of 2x2 Rib, work back and
forth in rows for 3", ending with RS facing. Change
to CC and k 1 row even. Work Row 1 (WS) of 2x2
Rib. BO in 2x2 Rib.
Weave in all ends.
Pin and back-
stitch zipper
in place
with
small sts.

knit wit

Unless you're proficient with a sewing
machine, sew zippers in by hand.
You'll have much more control and
can make subtle adjustments
as you go.

purple haze cardigan

DESIGNED BY JENNA WILSON

Elegance and coziness aren't enemies. In fact, they live happily together in this soft mohair cardigan. It's designed to be worn open, with the front edges hanging straight down. And look — no nasty neckline sag! But if you must wrap yourself in this sweater (and who could blame you?), knit the next larger size and shorten the body and sleeves to fit your measurements. Directions for a sleek tie belt are included.

The sweater calls for a double dose of Rowan yarns in complementary shades of soft violet—Kid Classic and Kidsilk Haze—knit together to create lightly fuzzy, silky, tone-on-tone lusciousness.

SIZE

XS[S, M, L, XL, XXL]

FINISHED MEASUREMENTS

Chest: 36[40, 44, 48, 52, 56]"
Length: 23.5[25, 25, 25.5, 27, 27.5]"

MATERIALS

Rowan Kid Classic [70% lambswool, 26% kid mohair, 4% nylon; 154yd/140m per 50g]; color: Royal 835; 8[8, 9, 10, 11, 11] skeins

Rowan Kidsilk Haze [70% super kid mohair, 30% silk; 230yd/210m per 25g]; color: Majestic 589; 5[6, 6, 7, 8, 8] skeins

Yarn quantities include sufficient yarn to knit optional belt.

1 set US #8/5mm straight needles
1 button, 0.5" diameter (optional)
Stitch holder
Yarn needle

GAUGE

18 sts/24 rows = 4" in St st with one strand of each yarn held together

STITCH PATTERNS

1x1 RIB (worked over odd number of sts):
RS: *K1, p1* to last st, k1.
WS: *p1, k1* to last st, p1.

TO DEC 1 ST AT THE BEG, END, OR BEG *AND* END OF A ROW:

Beg of a RS row: K1, ssk, work rem of row as instructed.

End of a RS row: Work to the last 3 sts of the row, k2tog, k1.

Beg of a WS row: P1, p2tog, work rem of row as instructed.

End of a WS row: Work to the last 3 sts of the row, ssp, p1.

PATTERN

Note: *Hold 1 strand of each yarn together throughout.*

BACK:

CO 109[121, 133, 145, 157, 169] sts. Beg with RS, work 4" in 1x1 Rib, ending with RS facing.
Next row: K2, (ssk, k2) to last 3 sts, ssk, k1. (82[91, 100, 109, 118, 127] sts)
P 1 row even.
Remainder of back will be worked in St st.
Work 5 rows even.
Next row: Dec 1 st at beg and end of row.
Work 7 rows even.
Next row: Dec 1 st at beg and end of row.
Rep last 8 rows once more. (76[85, 94, 103, 119, 121] sts)
Work 9[11, 11, 11, 13, 13] rows even.
Work inc row: K1, m1, work to last st, m1, k1.
Rep last 10[12, 12, 12, 14, 14] rows twice more. (82[91, 100, 109, 118, 127] sts)
Work 10 rows even.

Shape armholes:
BO 4[5, 5, 7, 8, 9] sts at beg of next 2 rows.
On next 0[2, 4, 4, 4, 6] rows, dec 1 st at beg and end of row. Work 1 row even.
Next row: Dec 1 st at beg and end of row.
Rep last 2 rows 1[1, 2, 2, 4, 4] times more.
Work 2 rows even.

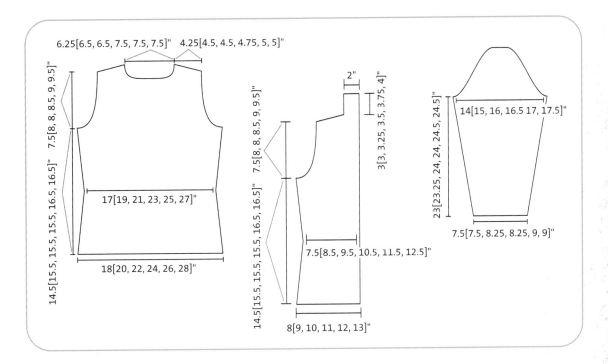

6.25[6.5, 6.5, 7.5, 7.5, 7.5]"   4.25[4.5, 4.5, 4.75, 5, 5]"

7.5[8, 8, 8.5, 9, 9.5]"

14.5[15.5, 15.5, 15.5, 16.5, 16.5]"

17[19, 21, 23, 25, 27]"

18[20, 22, 24, 26, 28]"

7.5[8, 8, 8.5, 9, 9.5]"

14.5[15.5, 15.5, 15.5, 16.5, 16.5]"

2"

3[3, 3.25, 3.5, 3.75, 4]"

7.5[8.5, 9.5, 10.5, 11.5, 12.5]"

8[9, 10, 11, 12, 13]"

14[15, 16, 16.5 17, 17.5]"

23[23.25, 24, 24, 24.5, 24.5]"

7.5[7.5, 8.25, 8.25, 9, 9]"

Next row: Dec 1 st at beg and end of row.
Rep last 3 rows 1[1, 1, 2, 2, 3] times more.
(66[69, 72, 75, 78, 79] sts)
Work even until piece measures 7.5[8, 8, 8.5, 9, 9.5]"
from beg of armhole shaping.

Shape shoulders:
BO 5 sts at beg of next row.
Work until 44[46, 48, 51, 52, 53] sts remain on
RH needle.
BO next 22[23, 24, 27, 26, 27] sts, work to end.
Place the first 22[23, 24, 24, 26, 26] sts worked
from this row on a holder.
Next row: BO 5 sts at beg of row and work to
neck edge. Dec 1 st at beg of next row, and work
to end. Rep last 2 rows 2[2, 2, 2, 1, 1] times more.
XL AND XXL SIZES ONLY: BO 4 sts at beg of
row and work to neck edge; dec 1 st at beg of next
row and work to end. Rep last 2 rows once more.

ALL SIZES: BO all rem sts and break yarn.
Return held sts to needles and join yarn at other
neck edge so that WS is facing for next row. Dec 1st
at beg of next row and work to end.
Next row: BO 5 sts at beg of row and work to
neck edge.
Next row: Dec 1 st at beg of row and work to end.
Rep last 2 rows 1[1, 1, 1, 0, 0] times more.
XL AND XXL SIZES ONLY: BO 4 sts at beg of row
and work to neck edge; dec 1 st at beg of next row
and work to end. Rep last 2 rows once more.
ALL SIZES: BO all rem sts and break yarn.

RIGHT FRONT:

CO 49[53, 59, 63, 71, 73] sts. Beg with RS, work 4" in 1x1 Rib, but slip the first st of every RS row knitwise instead of k it. End with RS facing.

Next row: Sl first st knitwise, continue working 1x1 Rib for another 11 sts, (ssk, k2) to last 9(1, 3, 3, 9, 1) sts, (ssk, k1) 3(0, 1, 1, 3, 0) times, k0(1, 0, 0, 0, 1). (39[43, 47, 50, 54, 58] sts)

Next row (WS): Purl across row until 12 sts remain on RH needle; work the last 12 sts in 1x1 Rib pattern as est.

Work 5 rows even as est.

Next row: Dec 1 st at beg of row.

Work 7 rows even.

Next row: Dec 1 st beg of row.

Rep last 8 rows once more.

(36[40, 44, 47, 51, 55] sts)

Work 9[11, 11, 11, 13, 13] rows even.

Next row: P1, m1, work to end.

Rep last 10[12, 12, 12, 14, 14] rows twice more.

(39[43, 47, 50, 54, 58] sts)

Work 11 rows even.

Shape armholes:

BO 4[5, 5, 7, 8, 9] sts at beg of next row.

On next 0[2, 4, 4, 4, 6] rows, dec 1 st at side edge.

Work 1 row even.

Next row: Dec 1 st at side edge.

Rep last 2 rows 1[1, 2, 2, 4, 4] times more.

Work 2 rows even.

Next row: Dec 1 st at side edge.

Rep last 3 rows 1[1, 2, 2, 2, 3] times more.

(31[32, 33, 33, 34, 34] sts)

Work even until armhole depth is the same as for back, ending with WS facing.

Shape shoulders:

BO 5 sts at beg of next row. Work 1 row even.

Rep last two rows 2[2, 2, 2, 1, 1] times more.

XL AND XXL SIZES ONLY: BO 4 sts at beg of every other row twice.

ALL SIZES:

Next row: BO sts until 12 sts (for center front edge) remain on LH needle.

Cont to work these 12 sts even in est patt for 3[3, 3.25, 3.5, 3.75, 4]", ending with RS facing.

Next row: Ssk 6 times: 6 sts rem. Place these sts on a holder.

LEFT FRONT:

CO 49[53, 59, 63, 71, 73] sts.

Beg with WS, work 4" in 1x1 Rib, but slip the last st of every RS row knitwise instead of knitting it. End with WS facing.

Next row: Work 1x1 Rib for 12 sts, *p2tog, p2, rep from * to last 9(1, 3, 3, 9, 1) sts, (p2tog, p1) 3(0, 1, 1, 3, 0) times, p0(1, 0, 0, 0, 1).

(39[43, 47, 50, 54, 58] sts)

Next row (RS): K across row until 12 sts remain on RH needle; work these 12 sts in 1x1 Rib pattern as previously est.

Work 5 rows even.

Next row: Dec 1 st at side edge.

Work 7 rows even.

Next row: Dec 1 st at side edge.

Rep last 8 rows once more. (36[40, 44, 47, 51, 55] sts)

Work 9[11, 11, 11, 13, 13] rows even.

Next row: K1, m1, work to end.

Rep last 10[12, 12, 12, 14, 14] rows twice more.

(39[43, 47, 50, 54, 58] sts)

Work 11 rows even.

Shape armholes:

BO 4[5, 5, 7, 8, 9] sts at beg of next row.

On next 0[2, 4, 4, 4, 6] rows, dec 1 st at side edge.

Work 1 row even

Next row: Dec 1 st at side edge. Rep last 2 rows 1[1, 2, 2, 4, 4] times more.

Work 2 rows even.

Next row: Dec 1 st at side edge. Rep last 3 rows 1[1, 1, 2, 2, 3] times more.

(31[32, 33, 33, 34, 34] sts])

Work even until armhole depth is the same as for back, ending with RS facing.

Shape shoulders:

BO 5 sts at beg of next row.

Work the next row even.

Rep last two rows 2[2, 2, 2, 1, 1] times more.

XL AND XXL SIZES ONLY:

BO 4 sts at beg of every other row twice.

ALL SIZES:

Next row: BO sts until 12 sts (for center front edge) remain on LH needle. Work these 12 sts even, in est pattern, for 3[3, 3.25, 3.5, 3.75, 4]", ending with WS facing.

Next row: P2tog 6 times: 6 sts rem. Place these sts on a holder or waste yarn.

SLEEVES (make two):

CO 45[45, 49, 49, 53, 53] sts. Beg with RS, work 2" in 1x1 Rib, ending with RS facing.

Next row: K1, pick up horizontal strand of yarn between the st just knit and the next st, and p1, k1 into this strand. Work in est 1x1 Rib pattern to last st, pick up horizontal strand of yarn between the st just purled and the next st, and k1, p1 into this strand, k1. (49[49, 53, 53, 57, 57] sts)

Work 11 more rows in 1x1 Rib pattern.

Remainder of sleeve will be worked in St st.

Work 5 rows even.

Inc row: K1, m1, work to last st, m1, k1.

Rep last 6 rows 0[3, 3, 5, 5, 7] times more. (51[57, 61, 65, 69, 73] sts)

Work 9[7, 7, 7, 7, 7] rows even.

Inc row: K1, m1, work to last st, m1, k1.

Rep last 10[8, 8, 8, 8, 8] rows 5[4, 4, 4, 3, 2] times more. (63[67, 71, 75, 77, 79] sts)

Work even until sleeve measures 16.5[16.75, 17, 17, 17, 17.5]" from beg.

Shape cap:

BO 4[5, 5, 7, 8, 9] sts at beg of next two rows.

Next 2 rows: Dec 1 st at beg and end of row.

Work 1 row even.

Next row: Dec 1 st at beg and end of row.
Rep last 2 rows 3[5, 2, 1, 1, 0] times more.
(43[41, 51, 53, 53, 55] sts)
Work 2 rows even.
Next row: Dec 1 st at beg and end of row.
Rep last 3 rows 3[1, 5, 7, 9, 10] times more.
Work 1 row even.
Next row: Dec 1 st at beg and end of row.
Rep last 2 rows 3[4, 3, 2, 0, 0] times more.
(27[27, 31, 31, 31, 31] sts)
On next 2 rows, dec 1 st at beg and end of row.
BO 3[3, 4, 4, 4, 4] sts at beg of next 2 rows.
BO 4[4, 5, 5, 5, 5] sts at beg of next 2 rows.
BO rem sts.

BELT (optional):
CO 12 stitches. On first row, (k1, p1) to end.
Next row: Sl 1 knitwise, (p1, k1) to last st, p1.
Rep this last row until the belt is as long as desired.
BO.

FINISHING

Block all pieces. Sew back to fronts at shoulders.
Join the collar extensions protruding from the fronts
either by grafting the live sts from the holder/waste
yarn from the right side, or by seaming on the
wrong side. Sew bottom edge of collar to back
neckline, stretching the collar gently to fit. Set and
sew sleeves in place on body. Sew sleeve and side
seams. Weave in and trim yarn tails.

knit wit

Purple haze is designed with set-in sleeves. Some people
find it tricky to sew a curved edge to a straight edge, but it's
easier than it sounds.

Fold the sleeve in half lengthwise to find the very center of the
top of the sleeve cap. Mark it temporarily with a safety pin. Match this
point to the shoulder seam on the body, and sew the center 2 inches of
the sleeve cap (1 inch on either side of the center point) to the top of the
shoulder (1 inch on either side of the shoulder seam). Now move to the
bottom of the sleeve cap, where you did your first BO rows of sleeve cap
shaping. Match the bottom inch or two on either end of the sleeve cap
to the bottom inch or two of the armhole on the body front and
back, and sew them in place. The curved portions of the sleeve
cap are attached next. Gently urge the curved edge of the
sleeve cap to meet the straight edge of the body, and
temporarily secure it in a few places with safety
pins or waste yarn. Then sew the rest
of the sleeve cap seam.

For wrap version: Sew button to
the wrong side of the right front at
waist level, about 2" in from the
edge where ribbing meets the
body. Single crochet a small loop
and attach it to the right side
of the left front at waist level,
about 2" in from the edge. Use
the button and loop to hold
the jacket closed, then tie the
belt over the top.

coral bikini

DESIGNED BY REBECCA HATCHER

This is a bikini. And it isn't.

See, it *is* a bikini if you wear the set to the beach. But wear the tank-style top alone with a pair of jeans, and you're quite ready for non-water-based activities. Both top and bottom are designed with welt-stitch scrunching in strategic places so you can adjust them to allow more or less coverage, depending on your mood. Excellent.

SIZE

S[M, L, XL]

Bust: 34[36, 38, 40]"

Hips: 33[35, 37, 39]"

FINISHED MEASUREMENTS

Chest: 28[30, 32, 34]" [unstretched]

Top length: 11[11.5, 12, 12.5]"

Low waist: 27[29, 31, 33]" [unstretched]

MATERIALS

Cascade Fixation [98.3% cotton/1.7% elastic; 100yd/92m [relaxed] per 50g]; color: 9210 Sunset; 4[5, 5, 6] balls

1 24" US#3/3.25mm circular needle

Yarn needle

Crochet hook

Stitch holder

GAUGE

31 sts/51 rows = 4" in St st (unstretched)

STITCH PATTERNS

WELT STITCH (in the round):

Rounds 1-4: P all sts.

Rounds 5-8: K all sts.

WELT STITCH (flat):

Rows 1, 3, 6, 8: K1, p across, k1.

Rows 2, 4, 5, 7: K all sts.

PATTERN

TOP:

CO 184[200, 216, 232] sts. PM and join. In the rnd, work 4 rows even in rev St st [p all sts]. Change to St st and work even until piece measures 1.5" from beg.

Next row: K 92[100, 108, 116], PM, k to end of rnd.

Midriff shaping:

K2, m1, *k to 2 sts before second marker, m1, k1.

Rep from * for second marker.

Work 9 rounds even in St st.

Rep these 10 rounds 4 times more.

(204[220, 236, 252] sts)

Cont even in St st until piece measures 6" from beg.

Bust shaping:

Working in St st, inc 10 sts evenly between markers, (this is now the front) slip marker, then k the rem 102[110, 118, 126] sts (this is the back). (214[230, 246, 262] sts)

Beg with Row 1, work Welt st patt across the front, working back half in St st.

At the same time, on Rows 1 and 5, work eyelet in the center of the front as foll:

Row 1: P 56[60, 64, 68], yo, p2tog, p 54[58, 62, 66].

Row 5: K 56[60, 64, 68], yo, k2tog, k 54[58, 62, 66].

Work 16 rows of Welt st patt, continuing to work eyelets in the center of Rows 1 and 5, and working the back even in St st. End at first marker. Place 102[110, 118, 126] sts just worked [back] on scrap yarn.

Working on the front only, work Rows 1-8 of the flat welt patt 5[6, 7, 8] times, then Rows 1-4 once more, continuing to work eyelets in Rows 1 and 5 as est. *At the same time,* dec 1 st at each end of every RS row. (68 sts) BO all sts.

STRAPS:

CO 70[75, 80, 85] sts. Beg at upper right corner of front, pick up 26[30, 34, 38] sts down slanted edge of top, k 102[110, 118, 126] sts across back, pick up 26[30, 34, 38] sts up slanted left edge of top [to upper left corner].

CO 70[75, 80, 85] sts. (294[320, 346, 372] sts) Do not join. Work 4 rows in rev St st, beg with k row. BO all sts.

BOTTOM

CO 200[216, 232, 248] sts. PM and join. P 3 rounds.

Next rnd: P 88[96, 104, 112], PM, p around to 1st marker.

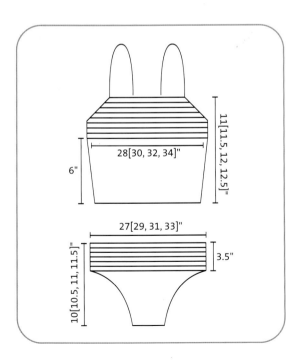

Next rnd: Beg welt patt in rnd, starting with a Row 5. *At the same time,* work eyelet in Rows 1 and 5 as foll:

Row 1: P to 2 sts before marker, yo, p2tog. Rep for 2nd marker.

Row 5: K to 2 sts before marker, yo, k2tog. Rep for 2nd marker.

Work welts and eyelets as established for 39 rows, ending with Row 3.

Shape legs:

Next rnd: P 191[206, 221, 236], BO 9[10, 11, 12]. Remove marker and BO 9[10, 11, 12] more sts. K70[76, 82, 88] and place on a holder [this will be the front], BO 18[20, 22, 24], k 94[100, 106, 112].

BACK:

On rem 94[100, 106, 112] sts, working flat in St st, dec 1 st at each end of every RS row as foll:

RS: K2, ssk, k to 4 sts from end, k2tog, k2.

WS: K1, p across, k1.

Rep these 2 rows until 16[18, 20, 22] sts rem, ending with RS row. Cut yarn, leaving short tail. Place rem sts on a holder.

FRONT:

Transfer the 70[76, 82, 88] sts from the front to the working needle. With RS facing, join yarn and work in St st, dec as for back until 16[18, 20, 22] sts rem. Continue in St st on these 16[18, 20, 22] sts [k the first and last st of each row as a selvedge] until piece measures 2.5[2.75, 3, 3.25]" from last decrease. Cut yarn, leaving 12" tail, and graft to the 16[18, 20, 22] sts from back.

FINISHING

Using yarn, and being careful not to tighten sts too much, sew cast-on edge of rev St st trim to inside of suit at waist of top and bottom. For top, sew cast-on edge to bound-off edge of strap, cont around back of top, and sew top front bound-off edge to inside.

Sew ends of straps to upper edge of back, spacing them evenly.

Using chain st, crochet three ties, two 15" long and one 18" long. Thread shorter ties through sides of bottom, and longer tie through center of top.

knit wit

Don't feel compelled to hold your needles and yarn in a particular way—and don't stop knitting because the way you were first shown to hold the needles isn't right for you. Your hands are strong and flexible (and weak and stiff) in their own way, so keep experimenting until you find something comfortable.

this part
is about me
and some other
nice people

acknowledgments

I thank my grandma, **Lillian Balaban Goldstein Bernstein**, for teaching me much more than how to knit, but especially that.

HarperCollins, for enabling.

The fine people at **Quirk: Sharyn**, for finding me; **Sarah**, for her enduring calm, patience, and skill; **Lynne**, for making us all look so superfine.

Erica, for getting the mojo right from the start.

The **23 talented designers** who put wit in the knit.

Kristi & **Kate**, for skillfully meshing the work of 24 different designers.

Extrahuge thanks to **my fairy gm**, for coming along at just the right time and saving my patoot.

Lisanne & **Bryce**, for laughter and good lighting.

Everyone who's supported Knitty and helped it grow.

Berroco, Cascade, Design Source, Lorna's Laces, Mission Falls, Nic Norman, and Westminster Fibers for their valuable support.

Rob & **Matt** at threadbearfiberarts.com, for producing instant yarn in time of crisis.

Pam Allen, for sharing.

Melanie Falick, for leading by example.

My knitting friends—**Kate, Jenna, Stephannie** & **Kathy**—for never telling me to shut up about the damned book already, plus all the good advice.

Jillian, for the pink Fixation and everything since.

My sister, **Jood**, and **my parents**, for a lifetime of love and support.

Newton, for being fuzzy and countless bunny kisses.

And to **Philly**, for all the yays. I love you.

meet the designers

VÉRONIK AVERY Véronik is a knitwear designer who lives with her husband and daughter in Montreal, Quebec. She found her true calling in her thirties after spending much of her early adulthood involved in fine arts photography and costume design. Her knitwear designs have been published in Melanie Falick's *Weekend Knitting* (Stewart, Tabori & Chang) and appear regularly in the magazine *Interweave Knits*. Her website can be found at www.veronikavery.com.

JAMIE COOK-JAQUES A web developer who lives and works in the Pacific Northwest, Jamie sketches most of her design ideas on pink post-it notes while she's on the job. When not knitting, she is learning to master her sewing machine, perusing eBay for good deals on yarn, or fretting over paint colors for her first home, which she shares with husband, Bob, and two cats, the Midget and Saity Bean. Find out more about Jamie's endeavors at www.TheRedSweater.com.

KAT COYLE Kat lives in sunny Los Angeles where she happily knits cotton skirts and lacy mohair shawls. See more of her work at www.katcoyle.com.

REBECCA HATCHER Rebecca lives near Boston, Massachusetts, with a rabbit that nibbles acrylics while ignoring wool, cotton, and other natural fibers. She learned to knit from her favorite grandmother when she was in elementary school. (When grandma took a nap halfway through the lesson, Rebecca figured out the rest on her own.) When not knitting, Rebecca runs marathons and eats cookies. To support her yarn, sneaker, and cookie habits, she works at a nonprofit center that helps libraries, archives, museums, and historical societies care for their paper-based materials.

ERICA HOHMANN Erica learned to knit about three years ago while attending Mount Holyoke College. She currently lives in a small town in central Massachusetts with her boyfriend and their pet fiddler crab, and works as an emergency medical technician.

STEFANIE JAPEL Stefanie's mother is an expert seamstress who taught her how to use a sewing machine as soon as she showed an interest. She immediately began making dog toys and outfitting dolls, and was sewing her own clothes before she got to high school. Stefanie learned the basics of knitting from her Grandma Reed by age eight, but she didn't really get started until her early twenties. She designs most of what she knits and writes about that process at www.glampyre.com.

MARIE-CHRISTINE MAHE Marie-Christine's grandmother tried to teach her to knit at an early age "to shut her up." This didn't work very well, but Marie-Christine enthusiastically took knitting up again after being exposed to a wild, improvised sweater. She launched her knitting design career with a project called the Vegan Fox published in *Knitty* magazine's inaugural issue; see www.knitty.com. She has since created an assortment of designs in a similar vein, which can be viewed at www.fuzzygalore.biz.

JILLIAN MORENO Jillian's yarn stash has its own room in Ann Arbor, Michigan.

SARAH MUNDY Sarah makes a lot of different things from her headquarters in Victoria, British Columbia. If you change the punctuation in knitting patterns, they look a lot like the software code she writes for a living. When she's not knitting or working, she grows food, provides sex education material to curious parties, and enthuses about pet toads, local rock stars and…most everything. The productive parts are catalogued at www.alohamedia.net.

LESLIE PETROVSKI Leslie is a full-time freelance writer who has been knitting since she was seven years old. Among other things, she writes for *Vogue Knitting*, teaches creative project classes at the Recycled Lamb in Lakewood, Colorado, and keeps up a blog called Nake-id Knits (www.radio.weblogs.com/0121658). When she's not writing or knitting or writing about knitting, she adores squeezing her two cats and husband, Mitch.

KRISTI PORTER Kristi enjoys knitting, but finds the greatest satisfaction in design work; her simple designs often use bright colors and fun yarns to make a splash. She enjoys rethinking and reworking conventional or already-made garments to create fresh new things. She is advertising manager for *Knitty* magazine—www.knitty.com—and a frequent contributor. She lives with her husband, Leo, and two daughters, Zoe and Eleanor, in San Diego, California.

MEGAN REARDON Megan made an attempt at learning to knit in college that involved ridiculously tight stitches and ended with balls of yarn being thrown out of the window. She took a few years to calm down and, once she got the hang of purling, she hasn't stopped since. She sells knitting needle cases at The Organized Knitter, www.organizedknitter.com.

STEPHANNIE ROY Just the other day, Stephannie finished her Ph.D. in Sociology and Equity Studies in Education at the University of Toronto (seriously). She wanted to knit a thesis, but her committee preferred she take the conventional approach. She plans to pursue a career in academia, but fantasizes about running away to a villa filled with DVDs and yarn.

Stephannie lives in Toronto with her husband, Craig, and their fabulous children, Emma and Alexander, who were trained as babies not to touch Mommy's knitting. You can read about her exploits on her blog (www.acunningplan.typepad.com/and-sheknitstoo).

CATHERINE SHU Catherine's mother taught her how to knit when she was five years old, and since then she has amassed a large stash of yarn that she stores in the form of a tangled lump. Since she stumbled upon the ballerina Suzanne Farrell's autobiography in her dorm's giveaway pile, Shu has been a Balanchine fan. When not indulging her raging balletomania, Catherine is a permanent intern—most recently at *The Village Voice*—freelance writer, and itinerant beader. She lives in New York City.

KAREN STOCKTON Karen lives in beautiful Kyoto, Japan, with her husband and cats, where she teaches high school English and frets over her tatami-mat flooring.

The sweet smell of reeds;
Hear the tatami mat shred
Cat running in house

AMY SWENSON Amy's overwhelming addiction to yarn is mostly paid for by her work as a business analyst. Since 2003, Amy has published her own line of original patterns, IndiKnits, that can be found in yarn shops across North America. She is also an active contributor to *Knitty*. More information on her knitwear designs can be found at www.indiknits.com.

IVETE TECEDOR Ivete lives in the suburbs of New York City with her dog and two roommates. She's been knitting since she was seven and keeps a knitting journal online at www.ivete.typepad.com/knotology. She dreams of the day when she can afford to knit all cashmere, all the time.

THERESA VINSON STENERSEN Learning to knit was an integral part of the successful transformation of Theresa's life a few years ago. Relocating to Norway from North Carolina was another. Climate shock hit hard and she soon got busy knitting thick woolen socks to keep her toes at the temperature to which they were accustomed.

Knitting and her weblog, Bagatell (www.spellingtuesday.com), have been essential in connecting Theresa to some wonderful people around the world, including the author of this book, who has opened up a world of opportunities and to whom she is entirely grateful.

MELISSA WALTERS Melissa has been knitting for more than 20 years. She lives in Maine with her husband, two children, and many pets. When she is not knitting and with her family, she works as a physician assistant at a busy health center. Her first designs included stirrup covers for her gyn exam table at work and a hammock for her daughter's pet rats.

JENNA WILSON Jenna lives and knits in Toronto. By day, she's a mild-mannered intellectual property lawyer, and by night she dabbles in knitwear design. Jenna's yarn stash—the result of years of careful hoarding—spans two cities and is the envy of her knitting friends, but a major inconvenience to her family. She chronicles random aspects of her knitting life at www.girlfromauntie.com.

NATALIE WILSON After an early knitting attempt that produced a pink garter-stitch cat, Natalie picked up the needles for good in the early 1990s. Designing knitwear for cash and fame fulfills Natalie's middle-school career goal of becoming a fashion designer. These days, from her Detroit-area base, Natalie designs for magazines, yarn companies, and her own iKnitiative line of patterns (www.iknitiave.com). She has also been a consulting environmental scientist for over 15 years, making good on her other middle-school career goal. Natalie's in-home fan club consists of a loving husband and two wonderful young children.

KATE WATSON Kate tries to hide from her growing reputation as a knitting numbers geek while attempting to be just grown-up enough to not seriously damage her children. In the winter, she's torn between loving her hometown of Toronto and despairing over her ancestors' decision that Canada is The Place To Be. She sincerely hates writing her own bios but quite enjoys speaking in third person.

KATHY WORTEL Kathy lives in Toronto with her husband, Rudy, daughter, Emma, and their Yorkshire terrier, Suki.

the sources

BERROCO, INC.
14 Elmdale Road, P.O. Box 367
Uxbridge, MA 01569
www.berroco.com

CASCADE YARNS
1224 Andover Park East
Tukwila, WA 98188
www.cascadeyarns.com

**CRYSTAL PALACE &
ASHFORD YARNS**
3006 San Pablo Avenue
Berkeley, CA 94702
www.straw.com

GGH YARNS
In the U.S., contact Muench
285 Bel Marin Keys Blvd., Unit J
Novato, CA 94949-5763
www.muenchyarns.com

In Canada, contact Estelle Designs
2220 Midland Avenue, Unit 65
Scarborough, ON M1P 3E6
info@estelledesigns.ca

KOIGU WOOL DESIGNS
RR# 1 Williamsford
Ontario, Canada N0H 2V0
www.koigu.com

LORNA'S LACES
4229 North Honore Street
Chicago, IL 60613
www.lornaslaces.net

**MANOS DEL URUGUAY
YARNS**
Contact Design Source
P.O. Box 770
Medford, MA 02155
781-438-9631

MISSION FALLS
*In the U.S., contact Unique
Kolours*
28 Bacton Hill Road
Malvern, PA 19355
www.uniquekolours.com

In Canada, contact Mission Falls
P.O. Box 224
Consecon ON K0K 1T0
www.missionfalls.com

NIC NORMAN
Custom belt buckles shown on
page 75.
www.nicnorman.com

PELSGARN
Contact Swedish Yarn Imports
P.O. Box 2069
126-A Wade Street
Jamestown, NC 27282

REXLACE
Contact Pepperell Braiding
Company
22 Lowell Street, P.O. Box 1487
Pepperell, MA 01463
978-433-2133
www.pepperell.com

ROWAN/JAEGER
Contact Westminster Fibers, Inc.
4 Townsend West, Unit 8
Nashua, NH 03063
603-886-5041
info@westminsterfibers.com

SCHACHENMAYR
*In the U.S., contact Knitting Fever
Inc.*
35 Debevoise Avenue
Roosevelt, NY 11575
www.knittingfever.com

In Canada
Visit www.diamondyarn.com

**TAHKI •
STACY CHARLES, INC.**
8000 Cooper Avenue, Building 1
Glendale, NY 11385
www.tahkistacycharles.com

TEJAS SUEDE LACE
Visit www.leatherfactory.com or
www.tandyleather.com

index

Italic page numbers refer to illustrations.

 all about me

Born in New Jersey, **AMY R. SINGER** has spent most of her life in Canada and likes it there. A professional editor and proofreader in the advertising industry since 1986, Amy is apparently wasting the Bachelor's degree in Radio & Television Arts she earned at Ryerson University. Most days, she'd really rather be knitting.

Thanks to the gentle patience of her grandma Lillian, Amy learned to knit when she was six. She vaguely remembers creating large, shapeless blobs of garter stitch, but has managed to block out the details. Allergic to wool, she has cultivated an intense appreciation for cotton in every form.

In the summer of 2002, Amy launched *Knitty* (www.knitty.com), a web-only knitting magazine with a sense of humor and absolutely no doily patterns. In early 2004, *Knitty* welcomed its millionth visitor. She also writes a column for *Interweave Knits* magazine about knitting and the internet. If she has any time left, she's probably fiddling with her new website, located at amysinger.ca

Other obsessions include sporadic attempts at fitness with a flat-water kayak or touring bike, and collecting vintage stuff. Amy lives in Toronto with her husband, Philip, and their mini-rex rabbit named Newton who grunts in her sleep.